CLAW
THIS JOURNAL

CLAW
THIS JOURNAL

An Activity Book for Cats
and Their Humans

SASSAFRAS LOWREY

CORAL GABLES

Cover Design: Elina Diaz
Cover Photo/illustration: Goodstudio/stock.adobe.com
Layout & Design: Elina Diaz

For permission requests, please contact the publisher at:
Mango Publishing Group
2850 S Douglas Road, 4th Floor
Coral Gables, FL 33134 USA
info@mango.bz

For special orders, quantity sales, course adoptions and corporate sales, please email the publisher at sales@mango.bz. For trade and wholesale sales, please contact Ingram Publisher Services at customer.service@ingramcontent.com or +1.800.509.4887.

Claw This Journal: An Activity Book for Cats and Their Humans

Library of Congress Cataloging-in-Publication number: Has been requested
ISBN: (print) 978-1-64250-965-6, (ebook) 978-1-64250-966-3
BISAC category code SEL045000, SELF-HELP / Journaling

Printed in China

For Thing, and in memory of all the cats who have bossed me around

TABLE OF CONTENTS

WELCOME CATS & CAT LOVERS!

If you're reading this book, chances are you are lucky enough to spend your life with at least one very special cat. The activities you'll find in this book involve training games, crafts, puzzle making, and more. The idea is to give you and your cat fun new ways to spend time together. It is my hope that you and your cats will enjoy this book as much as I have enjoyed writing it!

I've always loved cats; in fact, as with many people, my first pets were cats. When I was in elementary school, a friend and I had the idea to try to teach tricks to our cats. Our cats were tolerant, and our training skills weren't very effective, but I have always loved spending time with cats, and learning about how they experience the world. As a young adult, I got the first cat who was truly mine. Zoey was a very large, rambunctious kitten who had spent the first months of his life living in a backpack, being cared for by a group of homeless teenagers. He had gotten too big for his backpack, and I agreed to take him. Zoey fit right in with my dogs and taught me a lot about how to bond and care for cats in new ways.

Eighteen years ago, when my partner and I got together, my family grew and I became a parent to two very fluffy cats, Sierra and Noirchat. These two cats taught me how to be subservient to cats, and they moved cross-country with us twice and lived to be over twenty! My youngest cat, Thing, was a surprise addition to our family. One winter night, walking home to our Brooklyn apartment in a blizzard, we found a tiny kitten. With the help of some dog treats in my pocket and cat food generously brought by owner of the bodega across the street we were able to catch the five-week-old black kitten with a broken tooth. Now, eight years later, Thing is a healthy, happy, inquisitive, and mischievous cat who enjoys playing, begging for food, and spending time learning new things. Thing has been an active collaborator in writing this book!

One of my greatest passions is helping people to better understand their pets and have more fun playing with them. Cats might have a reputation for being lazy or anti-social, but any of us who love cats know that isn't the case! Cats are inquisitive and intelligent. Cats are deeply bonded to their families and love engaging in play with their people. This book is all about showing you and your cats new ways to engage them in interactive games and play. Many of the enrichment activities you'll find in this book utilize your cat's natural instincts to sniff, scratch, paw, climb, and explore. These activities aren't about trying to control cats or tell them what to do—good luck with that! Rather, this book is filled with activities, games, and projects for you and your cats to do together. The idea behind these activities is to give your cats a more enriched life and help you find ways to understand your cat better and have more fun together!

—Sassafras & Thing

CAT TRAINING

Cats have a reputation for being untrainable, but that isn't the case! Even though some people might think that cat training sounds silly, or even impossible, that isn't the case at all. Cats are very intelligent and enjoy having opportunities to spend time with their people, learning new things. Cats love to learn; the key is finding what motivates your cat. Just like you want to get paid in money for going to work, your cat also is looking for payment or reinforcement, usually in the form of treats or play. Spending time training your cat can help you deepen the bond you have. Training isn't about making your cat do what you want—instead, training is about helping you and your cat develop a shared language and strengthen your ability to communicate and understand one another. When we are training cats, there are a variety of techniques you can utilize to help them learn. Techniques we will utilize at different points in the book include:

Shaping—With shaping, your cat is getting to put together the pieces of a trick without you prompting or leading them. Shaping works well with clicker training because it allows you to closely mark specific behavior changes or engagement with an object. In shaping, your cat is actively thinking and puzzling out a behavior, which can be rewarding and confidence-building for your cat.

Clicker Training—One method of training that works well for all kinds of animals, from cats to goldfish (yes, really!), is clicker training. Clicker training allows you to elicit a desired behavior and then provide a reward for it. The clicker is a little box-shaped plastic device you can get at most pet supply stores, which makes a metallic "click" noise when pressed. Clickers work because you can use one to clearly mark a precise movement or behavior, and then reward with a treat. Cats do well with clicker training because it allows us to clearly communicate with them.

Luring—Luring involves using a treat or a toy to lead your cat into the desired position. Luring is a fast and easy way to teach your cat a lot of tricks because it enables you to lead your cat into the desired position or behavior, and then attach a verbal or physical cue. When your cat is following a lured treat with their nose, the body follows, and so they end up in the position you want them in. As your cat gets more familiar with the skill, you can phase out the physical lure.

Capturing—This isn't always the fastest way to teach your cat a trick, but it can be extremely effective for teaching skills and tricks that are physically subtle, or behaviors that your cat does naturally. To teach a skill via capturing, you will be clicking or verbally marking a behavior each time you see them do it. With time and repetition, your cat will figure out that they are being treated or rewarded for the behavior they are doing, and then you can attach a verbal marker to that behavior so you can cue your cat to do it in the future.

We will explore these training modalities at various points in the book. The most important thing when training any animal, including cats, is that training sessions are fun and enjoyable for the leader.

ENGAGEMENT IS IMPORTANT

One of the primary themes that will come up a lot in this book is the idea of providing enrichment to our cats. Simply put, enrichment is providing activities for our cats that gives them options and choices and works with species-specific interests and behaviors. Providing your cat with opportunities to play, explore, and get both physical and mental exercise is important for their overall well-being. Cats who are getting enough attention, exercise, and enrichment are more likely to be happy, relaxed cats and may even be better behaved! It's been shown that bored cats are more likely to display behavioral problems than cats whose social, physical, and emotional needs are being met. In addition, providing enrichment for your cat is a whole lot of fun, and a great way for you and your cat to bond!

What do you and your cat most enjoy doing together?

_____

_____

_____

_____

_____

_____

_____

_____

_____

_____

_____

_____

_____

_____

_____

_____

PURR-SONALITY QUIZ

To help you understand your cat and get a better idea of what activities your cat might most enjoy participating in, take this purr-sonality quiz for your cat! As you go through the quiz, pick the answer that you think would best fit your cat. There are no right or wrong answers! Just answer honestly for how you think your cat would respond.

1. My cat's favorite activity is

    A. Hiding

    B. Napping

    C. Playing

    D. Cuddling

    E. Exploring

2. When my cat hears a loud noise, they

    A. Run and hide

    B. Ignore it

    C. Try to pounce on or chase the sound

    D. Seek me for attention

    E. Approach the sound

3. When friends or family come over, my cat

    A. Avoids visitors

    B. Keeps napping

    C. Brings out the toys

    D. Finds a lap

    E. Comes to investigate

4. When the treats come out, my cat

    A. Quietly watches

    B. Waits for me to bring it to him

    C. Comes to investigate

    D. Rubs on me for more

5. If a bug is in my house, my cat responds like

    A. Meoooow—save me!

    B. You gonna get that?

    C. Oh, a new toy!

    D. Let's watch that together.

    E. I'm gonna follow that for a while.

6. When my cat sees a toy, they respond like

    A. OMG, is that thing going to eat me?!

    B. Have fun with that.

    C. Woohoo!!!

    D. But what if we snuggled instead?

    E. Ohhhh, let's check this out!

7. On an average day, my cat spends most of their time

    A. Hiding

    B. Napping

    C. Playing

    D. Cuddling

    E. Exploring

8. If I'm just hanging out, my cat is

    A. Studiously ignoring me

    B. Sleeping

    C. Zoom, bang, ow!

    D. Trying to sit on top of me

    E. Studiously observing me

Look at your cat's answers and write down how many times you answered with each of the following letters:

    A. _____

    B. _____

    C. _____

    D. _____

    E. _____

PURR-SONALITY CAT-EGORIES

How did your cat score? This purr-sonality quiz is of course just for fun and isn't actually scientific. The idea behind putting cats into CAT-egories is to help you to get a better idea of what kinds of things your cat might enjoy doing. Obviously, each cat is an individual and likely fits partly in several temperament categories, but, for fun, we're going to think about categories.

A = Bashful Bobcat—These are cats who tend to be a little shyer and more reserved in their interactions.

B = Lounging Lion—These lazy kitties are always up for a good nap. All cats spend most of their day sleeping, but these cats are champion snoozers.

C = Playful Panther—These playful kitties are always ready for a game. Everything has the potential to be a toy for these cats!

D = Tender Tiger—Always ready for a snuggle, these cuddly cats are happiest when they are able to spend time with you.

E = Curious Cougar—Every day is an adventure for these inquisitive kitties. Always into things, these cats are always ready to explore.

As you work your way through the activity book, you'll see that each activity is labeled with one (or more) of these categories. This isn't intended to be prescriptive, but rather to help you get an idea for where you want to start, and just to give you a sense of things your cat might enjoy. Although many cats will have one category they most align with, most will be a mixture, so look at categories your cat scored high in when selecting activities to start doing with your cat. Keep in mind, though, that your cat might enjoy or excel at activities not identified with their purr-sonality result!

HOW TO USE THIS BOOK

Welcome! This book belongs to you and your cat. Despite the name, you probably don't want to let your cat claw the journal up. Beyond that, there really is no wrong way for you and your cat to enjoy and use this book. You can go through the activities in order, or you can skip around between different activities that interest you, or that you think your cat would like best.

This book is designed for you to write in and is interactive, so don't be afraid to personalize it! My hope is that you will make the book your own: break the spine, doodle on the margins, take notes on pages, paste in pictures of your cat—really, there is no wrong way to use this book, as long as you are having fun.

Some cats will be more interested in some activities than others, and that's okay! You and your cat don't have to do every activity in the book—just start by focusing on the activities that look like the most fun for you and your cat. The primary goal of this activity book is to support you and your cat having more fun together. Spending quality time with your cat is a great way to improve your bond and relationship. It's also about creating habits of enrichment where you and your cat build routines together through various activities and challenges. My hope is that you and your cat will explore some new things, and maybe discover something you really enjoy in the pages of this book.

There are already so many things about our cat's daily lives that we control, things we do because we need to, for safety or because of our lifestyle. When we focus on doing enriching activities with our cats, I think it's important that our cats have a lot of input into what we do and don't do. If there's an activity that isn't fun for your cat, don't do it! Not all cats like the same things, and not all cats have the same capacities or interests, and that's okay.

QUIZ ABOUT CATS

Do you think you're a cat expert? Take this quiz to test your cat knowledge. Some of the answers might surprise you!

1. When your cat rubs against you, it's because they own you. **TRUE or FALSE**

2. Cats are sweet, so they love sugar! **TRUE or FALSE**

3. Cats can recognize the sound of your voice. **TRUE or FALSE**

4. There are over thirty muscles in a cat's ears that let them independently rotate. **TRUE or FALSE**

5. Cats use their whiskers to measure space. **TRUE or FALSE**

6. Dogs are more popular than cats in the United States. **TRUE or FALSE**

7. A cat's nose has a unique print. **TRUE or FALSE**

8. Cats spend half their life grooming. **TRUE or FALSE**

9. Cats can have extra toes. **TRUE or FALSE**

10. Purrs can be healing. **TRUE or FALSE**

11. A group of cats is called a pride. **TRUE or FALSE**

12. Cats have more adult teeth than baby teeth. **TRUE or FALSE**

13. Cats' whiskers function like radar. **TRUE or FALSE**

14. The first cat show in the United States was held in New York City. **TRUE or FALSE**

15. The first record of cats being kept as pets is from ancient Egypt. **TRUE or FALSE**

16. Cats are small tigers. **TRUE or FALSE**

ANSWERS

1. **TRUE!** Rubbing against you may in part be a sign of affection, but it's also a way to show ownership of you. Cats mark their territory using scent glands on their paws, and on their head, so when your cat is rubbing against you, they are marking you as belonging to them.

2. **FALSE!** Cats actually can't taste sugar or sweetness.

3. **TRUE!** Cats recognize the sound of their human's voice and form close relationships with their families.

4. **TRUE!** There are thirty-two muscles in each of your cat's ears that allow them to rotate their ears independently 180 degrees!

5. **TRUE!** Cats use their whiskers to gain information about the world around them, including whether their body will fit through a space.

6. **FALSE!** Although it depends on who you ask, technically, cats are more popular pets in the United States. There are 88.3 million cats (according to a 2020 American Pet Products Association Survey) and 74.8 million dogs.

7. **TRUE!** Just like your fingerprint, a cat's nose print is unique to that individual cat.

8. **TRUE!** Experts estimate that cats can spend up to half their waking hours grooming themselves. Though not all cats' grooming routines are that elaborate, it's not uncommon.

9. **TRUE!** Polydactyl refers to a genetic mutation that causes cats to have "extra" toes on their paws. The majority of cats have five toes on each of their two front feet, and four on each of their back feet; however, polydactyl cats have extra toes, often six, on some or all of their paws.

10. **TRUE!** We might find our cat's purr soothing, and we aren't alone! Cats can engage in self-soothing purring when they are sick or aren't feeling well.

11. **FALSE!** A group of domestic cats is called a clouder.

12. **TRUE!** Kittens have twenty-six baby teeth, sometimes called milk teeth, but when their adult teeth come in, they have thirty permanent teeth.

13. **TRUE!** Cats' whiskers are connected to their nervous systems and function a bit like radar, allowing them to sense and detect shifts in their surroundings.

14. **FALSE!** Although the National Cat Show first took place in New York City's Madison Square Garden, May 8–11, 1895, and is viewed by many cat fanciers as the first cat show, there are actually records of cat shows happening in the 1870s in Boston.

15. **FALSE!** Although many historians believed that it was the ancient Egyptians who first kept domestic cats as pets, there is now evidence that the practice of keeping pet cats is even older! On the island of Cyprus, scientists have found the 9,500-year-old grave of a cat that had been buried with people, among their personal belongings. This grave would be more than 4,000 years older than the oldest cat burials found in Egypt.

16. **TRUE!** Our domestic cats share 95.6 percent of their genetics with tigers!

TIPS FOR GETTING STARTED

This book belongs to you and your cat! There are no wrong ways to use it. Don't stress about doing every activity, or how quickly you work your way through the activities. The goal is to spend more quality time with your cat and provide more enrichment in your cat's days. Training and playing with your cat shouldn't ever involve punishment or coercion. We want our cats to be enthusiastic learners and participants in the activities that we do together. Just as you want to get paid for going to work, we want to make sure to pay our cats for a job well done while we work on the activities in the book.

YOUR CAT

TREATS

As you and your cat are getting started with this journal, it's important to spend a little time thinking about what your cat finds most motivating and to spend some time thinking about the things your cat likes most. These are the kinds of activities and rewards we will be using for rewards and encouragement while training and while engaging our cats in different games. Rewards—generally treats, food, and/or toys—are what we'll use to motivate and reward our cat for participating in these activities. Just as you get a paycheck for going to work, we want to always "pay" our cats for learning something new or participating in games and activities. Using treats while training isn't bribing our cats to engage with us; rather, it's helping us build understanding and motivation for them. When we give our cats treats as part of training or playing, we communicate to them that they have done something we liked, which makes it more likely that they will offer the same movement or behavior in the future.

Just like us, cats have varying taste preferences when it comes to treats. For this section, take some time to experiment with different treats and see what your cat loves, what your cat likes, and what your cat maybe will eat, but isn't all that thrilled about. Some cats have preferences regarding the texture of treats, with some kitties preferring soft ones while others crave something chewy or crunchy. Other cats might prefer a treat that is soft and lickable. Our goal with this activity is to understand a little more about what treats are the most motivating for our cats. The treats your cat loves we will consider "high-value." This is what you want to use when you are asking your cat to engage in an activity that is new or challenging.

Cat treats are commercially available in a variety of textures and flavors that can all work well, depending on your cat's preferences. You can also try very small bits of unseasoned cooked meat, string cheese, or hot dogs. As your cat tries different treats, keep track of their preferences in this chart.

Eats	Likes	Loves

FAVORITE TOYS

If you love your cat, chances are you have purchased a lot of cat toys; sometimes your cat will play with them, and other times they might seem to have more fun playing with the packaging! Most cats enjoy opportunities to play, both independently and with their people. Playing with toys purchased, found, or crafted can provide cats with important physical and mental exercise. Toys can help cats channel their hunting instincts and prevent boredom. In addition, toys and toy-inspired play can improve your bond and relationship with your cat, and be a fun reward to offer your cat while you work through the activities in this book.

What toys does your cat like best? A kitten or cat's preferences for toys can change over time, so it's useful to return to this activity periodically to see how your cat's preferences for toys— or even different kinds of toys—may have changed.

Date	Date
Favorite Toys	Favorite Toys

Date	Date
Favorite Toys	Favorite Toys

Date	Date
Favorite Toys	Favorite Toys

Date	Date
Favorite Toys	Favorite Toys

FAVORITE GAMES

Do you and your cat have special games that you enjoy playing together? Common modalities of play that are enriching for cats include chasing, simulated hunting and fishing activities, and opportunities to explore. Some cats also enjoy gentle wrestling with their people's hands, or even retrieving thrown toys. Knowing what games your cat enjoys playing can help you make the most of the quality time you have to spend with your cat, especially on those days when, because of work, you might have limited time at home.

It's easy to get into a play rut and just play the same games over and over with your cat. Although most cats will have a favorite type of game, most kitties also enjoy getting variety in their play style. Don't be afraid to mix up your play routine and see what your cat enjoys! Use the space below to record what your cat thinks of different styles of play.

My Cat's Favorite Game Is:

_____

_____

_____

Chasing Games (e.g., chasing you, or a thrown toy):

My Cat's Reaction:

_____

_____

_____

Hunting Games (e.g., fishing pole toys that stimulate a cat's instinct to hunt):

My Cat's Reaction:

_____

_____

_____

Fishing Games (e.g., using their paws to "fish" toys or treats out of containers)

My Cat's Reaction:

_____

_____

_____

Exploring (e.g., empty boxes or paper bags):

My Cat's Reaction:

_____

_____

_____

DECIPHERING MEOWS

Does your cat meow to communicate what they want and need? Some cats are chattier than others. Cats communicate a lot of how they are feeling through body language as well as vocalizations. Cats make a variety of vocalizations, including meows, yowls, and purrs. Chances are, if you and your cat spend a lot of time together, you'll have a pretty good idea what your cat is trying to communicate. For example, my cat Thing makes his desire for meals extremely clear!

Pay attention to the vocalizations your cat makes in different situations or at different times of day. Below, you can keep track of your cat's meows, what is going on when they start vocalizing, and what you think the English translation might be!

Meow Situation:

_____

_____

Suspected Translation:

_____

_____

Meow Situation:

_____

_____

Suspected Translation:

_____

_____

Meow Situation:

_____

_____

Suspected Translation:

_____

_____

Meow Situation:

_____

_____

Suspected Translation:

_____

_____

Meow Situation:

_____

_____

Suspected Translation:

_____

_____

Meow Situation:

_____

_____

Suspected Translation:

_____

_____

Meow Situation:

_____

_____

Suspected Translation:

_____

_____

ABOUT MY CAT

1. My cat's birthday or gotcha day is: _____

2. My cat and I met (where/when): _____

3. My cat's breed (known or guessed) is: _____

4. My cat's favorite treat is: _____

5. My cat loves it when we: _____

6. My cat's favorite person is: _____

7. My cat's least favorite person is: _____

8. My cat's favorite toy is: _____

9. If my cat was a person and had a job, it would be: _____

10. If my cat was a politician, they would be: _____

11. My cat's worst habit is: _____

12. My cat is scared of: _____

13. My cat's best friend is: _____

14. The weirdest thing my cat does is: _____

15. My cat's favorite game is: _____

16. The funniest thing about my cat is: _____

FIRST MEETING

Do you remember when you saw your cat for the first time? Were you swiping through the online profiles of adoptable cats? Wandering the rows of adoptable cats at your local Humane Society? Did you know your cat's mother and littermates? Did you find your cat abandoned and know you needed to bring them home? Or did your cat choose you? There is no wrong way to meet the cat of your dreams, but most of us will never forget meeting our cat for the first time! Use this section to record special memories about finding your kitty companion.

Write the story of how you first met your cat:

_____

_____

_____

How old was your cat?

_____

If you didn't go alone to meet your cat, who was with you?

_____

How did you meet your cat?

_____

_____

_____

What was your cat like when you first met?

_____

_____

_____

What was your favorite thing about your cat when you met?

_____

_____

_____

Was there anything about your cat you were nervous or unsure about?

_____

_____

_____

What was your cat doing when you first met?

_____

_____

_____

What was it like bringing your cat home for the first time?

_____

How did your cat react to your house?

What are some of the first things you and your cat did together?

YOUR CAT'S FAVORITE ACTIVITIES

Just like us, cats have different things that they enjoy doing. Some cats, when not being entertained by their people, will go in search of things around the house to play with, while others will occupy themselves with a nap in a nice quiet space. Other very social cats will make it their mission to find a lap anywhere in the home to sit on and cuddle. What are your cat's favorite things to do (napping, eating, playing, cuddling etc.)?

My cat's favorite thing to do is:

_____

_____

Include a picture of your cat doing their favorite activity here:

MY CAT'S DAILY ROUTINE

Does your cat have a daily routine? It's true that cats can sleep, on average, between fifteen and twenty hours a day! That's a lot of time spent napping, but sleep isn't all that cats get up to. Cats are highly bonded to their people and tend to adapt their own natural schedules to match ours and maximize the amount of quality time they can spend with us. When they are young kittens, most cats are especially active and will generally start to slow down as they mature and reach adulthood. Cats are crepuscular, meaning that in general, as a species, they are naturally most active at dawn and dusk.

Are there times of day when your cat is most active?

_____

_____

Does your cat tend to wake up and demand breakfast at a certain time? Does your cat sleep in certain areas of the home at specific times of day—possibly because it's where you are or where the best sunbeams are coming through the windows? Does your cat come to bed with you at night? In the space below, write out your cat's daily routine:

Morning:

_____

_____

_____

_____

Afternoon:

_____

_____

_____

_____

Evening:

_____

_____

_____

_____

Night:

_____

_____

_____

_____

ACTIVITY TRACKER

How many steps do you think your cat takes in a day? Just as many of us now wear activity trackers or smart watches that track how much we walk in a day, it's now possible to get an activity tracker for your cat! Some of these trackers have built-in GPS devices, so you can track your cat if they are ever lost outside. The trackers can also track how many steps per day your cat takes.

Does your cat have an activity tracker?

How many steps per day does your cat take?

ADVOCACY

Is your cat shy? Not all cats are social butterflies—in fact, many cats tend to be a bit shy, especially when they are meeting new people. Everyone loves to watch cat videos online, and sometimes that leads people to assume that all cats are social or will want to form a connection with every cat they see or meet. Everyone loves to watch cat videos online, and sometimes that leads people to assume that all cats are social or will want to form a connection with them.

It can be tempting to try to gently push or encourage your cat to meet or interact with your friends and family when they come over, but putting them into stressful situations they don't feel ready for isn't a good way to help them bond with other people. It's perfectly okay to be a scaredy cat and prefer not to engage with visitors in the home. To help your cat be comfortable with guests, it's important to be their advocate and explain to people what will make your cat comfortable. For example, if you know your cat is nervous about people, you may want to ask guests to ignore the cat when they come into your home, and to let your cat take the lead on any engagement. Or, you might request that people only pet them on certain parts of their body or play with them only in certain ways. In any event, it's important to advocate for your cat and to ensure they are comfortable while you entertain friends or family.

Unfortunately, some people think it's funny when a cat runs to hide, hisses, or swipes when pursued by a guest, but these are signs that your cat is stressed and upset, which isn't funny at all. It might feel a little uncomfortable to tell people how to engage with your cat, but it's important to support your pet. You might be surprised—the more space you give your cat not to engage with guests, the more they may choose to!

Does your cat like visitors?

What does your cat do when people come over to your house?

_____

_____

_____

What are some things that make your cat unhappy, nervous, or uncomfortable?

_____

_____

_____

When do these situations come up?

_____

_____

_____

How does your cat react in these situations?

_____

_____

_____

What do you do?

_____

_____

_____

Are there ways you could intervene before your cat gets stressed, upset, or nervous?

_____

_____

_____

One of the hardest parts of advocating or standing up for your cat is knowing what to say. It can help a lot to practice in advance and have a script well-rehearsed.

What are some things you can say to people who want to do something that will make your cat uncomfortable?

_____

_____

_____

Practice helps! Even if you feel uncomfortable at first, the more you practice advocating for your cat's comfort, the more natural it will feel.

Do you notice any difference in your cat's confidence or behavior since you have started more intentionally advocating for your cat?

_____

_____

_____

GOAL SETTING

Do you want to have a better relationship with your cat? Do you wish you understood your cat better? One of the best ways to strengthen the relationship you have with them is to be intentional about the time you spend together. Maybe you want to spend more time grooming them or playing with them, instead of just sitting on the couch together every night after work.

These don't need to be big bucket-list-style goals; they can be smaller goals, like playing with your cat every morning before leaving for work or cleaning the litter box daily. Maybe you want to teach your cat to come when you call or to find new games to play that you both enjoy. Many behavioral challenges that people have with cats can be prevented by making sure that cats get more exercise and enrichment. The best way to deepen or build a better relationship with your cat is to set some goals. While setting goals, try to keep your plans realistic—stick to things you have the time to do—and then outline simple steps you can take to achieve that goal.

What do you wish was different in your relationship with your cat?

_____

_____

_____

What steps can you take to achieve that goal?

1.

2.

3.

What is something you wish your cat did differently?

_____

_____

_____

What steps can you take to achieve that goal?

1.

2.

3.

What is something your cat wishes you did differently?

_____

_____

_____

What steps can you take to achieve that goal?

1.

2.

3.

What is something you and your cat can work on together?

_____

_____

_____

What steps can you take to achieve that goal?

1.

2.

3.

LIVING THE DREAM

You don't have to wait until New Year's Eve to set resolutions for the year to come. In fact, it's probably best not to wait! It's estimated that over 50 percent of New Year's resolutions end up getting abandoned—yikes! Those aren't great odds. Although New Year's resolutions often don't get adhered to, that doesn't mean it's impossible to change your behavior or the way you interact with your cat. I have a coffee cup in my kitchen that says, "I work hard to give my cat a better life." Often, because they can be somewhat independent, people will passively coexist with their cats instead of making their needs and comfort a priority. What kind of life do you and your cat have together? What kind of life do you wish the two of you had?

What kind of life do you want to have with your cat?

_____

_____

_____

What do you want to do more of?

_____

_____

_____

Do you have any regrets about what you have you done with your cat?

_____

_____

_____

If yes, what have you done and what can you do to change that in the future?

_____

_____

_____

What are your dreams with your cat?

_____

_____

_____

What areas of life with your cat do you want to be more intentional about?

_____

_____

_____

If your cat could talk, what do you think they would say about your life together?

_____

_____

_____

If you spent ten, fifteen, twenty, or thirty minutes a day intentionally focused on your cat, what would you want to spend that time doing?

_____

_____

_____

NAME GAME!

Names have power, and choosing the right name for a new cat or kitten who comes into your life is a big decision!

Does your cat know their name? YES   NO

Did you name your cat, or did someone else name them?

_____

_____

_____

What is the story or symbolism behind your cat's name?

_____

_____

_____

If you named your cat, how did you decide on their name?

_____

_____

_____

Did you know right away that was your cat's name, or did it take you a while to decide?

_____

_____

_____

Humans say a lot of things, and our cats understandably tune out a lot of our dialogue, but we want them to recognize their names and know when we are talking about them! If your cat doesn't know their name, or you aren't sure if they recognize that their name refers to them, it's fun and easy to spend some time working on name recognition with your cat.

Supplies Needed:

- 🐈 Treats your cat is excited about
- 🐈 Clicker (if you are clicker training)

Step 1: Start when your cat is awake and interested in engaging with you. Have your treats ready.

Step 2: Say your cat's name and immediately give them a treat. Repeat several times in a row. The goal here is to help your cat to make the association between hearing their name and good things happening.

Step 3: By pairing treats with your cat's name, they will start to pay special attention to that word and begin to understand that their name refers to them. Now, again with treats at the ready, say their name and then wait for them to look toward you, then use your verbal reward marker (like "yes"), or click if you are clicker training, and give your cat a treat.

Step 4: The more you practice with this game, the more your cat will associate the sound of their name with turning their attention toward you. As you play the name game, giving them treats for turning toward you, you can start to say their name while they are in another room or doing something. When you say your cat's name and they turn toward you, praise or click and give lots of treats.

> **Training Tip:** We always want to make sure that our cat has a positive association with their name. Never use your cat's name in an angry, scolding, or upset tone!

GROWING TOGETHER

Cats change our lives in a variety of ways. Cats give us important companionship, and they also make us kinder, and more thoughtful and responsible people. Cats keep us company when we are lonely, and, for many of us, they have shifted our daily routines and outlook in positive ways.

How has your cat changed your life?

_____

_____

_____

What is something you do, now that you have a cat, that you would never have done before?

_____

_____

_____

Was it hard to have your cat at first?

_____

_____

_____

How has that gotten easier over time?

_____

_____

_____

What do you wish you had known before bringing your cat home?

_____

_____

_____

What about having a cat is different from what you thought it would be like?

_____

_____

_____

What are the things you think about now that you wouldn't have before you brought a cat home?

_____

_____

_____

How have you as a person changed since you brought your cat home?

_____

_____

_____

How has your cat changed since you brought them home?

_____

_____

_____

NATURAL INSTINCTS

The cats we share our home and hearts with are domesticated, but cats retain natural instincts that helped keep their ancestors safe and well fed.

SCRATCHING

One behavior many cat owners struggle with is their cat scratching furniture and carpets. Although to some people scratching is a "nuisance" behavior, it is a natural instinct for cats and should be encouraged in appropriate locations. For cats, scratching is a way to mark territory and communicate. Cats have scent glands on their feet, and they can deposit scent from those glands by scratching. Cats may increase their scratching during times of stress, like a change in the family schedule, new family members, other animals hanging out outside your windows (or fire escapes if you're in an apartment), rearranged furniture, or moving.

Does your cat enjoy scratching? _____

Are there times when you notice your cat is scratching more? _____

In what locations around your home do you want your cat to scratch (e.g. cat tree, scratching post, scratching box, etc.)? _____

SCENT MARKING

After a long day, does your cat jump onto your lap and start rubbing you with their face? This may feel like a bit of a hug, and for cats, it's a way to demonstrate how much you mean to them. Cats have scent glands on their faces, and rubbing on you (or on the edges of furniture or walls) is a way for your cat to mark you as belonging to them—it's like a cat-scented hug!

Does your cat rub their face against you? _____

What other places does your cat rub their face against? _____

CLIMBING

Climbing is an extremely natural behavior for cats. Cats climb in order to get a better look at what is happening around them and to search for prey while hunting, as well as to hide and stay safe from predators. Climbing is pleasurable, fun, and comforting for cats, so it's important to provide our indoor cats with safe opportunities to climb in the home.

Does your cat enjoy climbing? _____

What kinds of things does your cat like to climb? _____

HUNTING

Cats are natural predators and skilled hunters. While our cats aren't hunting for their meals, the act of hunting is highly pleasurable and enriching for cats. Simulated hunting opportunities with toys are important for cats, and many cats will also invent hunting-like games with things they find around the house, like bugs, pen caps, hair ties, etc.

Do you ever find your cat "hunting" bits of trash, small bugs, or toys in
the house? _____

What are some of your cat's favorite things to "hunt"? _____

RUNNING WATER

Many cats seek out access to fresh running water regardless of how often you change the water in their bowl. This can lead to cats seeking out running water in showers, bathtubs, or sinks. Depending on what kind of faucet you have, some cats can even learn to turn on the tap themselves! In addition to drinking the water, some cats enjoy batting at and playing with it. An alternative option is to provide our cats with a cat fountain instead of a water dish—this allows them constant access to moving water without wasting water by leaving the sink running.

Does your cat like to drink out of a dripping faucet? _____

Have you ever gotten your cat a water fountain? _____

Does your cat like to play with running water? _____

MAKE AN EMERGENCY KIT

None of us like to think about disasters striking, but unfortunately, they are a scary part of our world. Natural disasters like hurricanes, earthquakes, and wildfires can impact anyone. It's important to think about how you will prepare for an emergency and include your cat in your disaster preparedness plans. If a natural disaster were to strike in your area, do you have everything your cat would need if you had to shelter in your home for an extended period of time, or if you had to evacuate?

Emergency Supply Kit

- Pet first-aid kit
- Dry/canned food (enough for at least a week)
- Bottled water
- Medication(s) your cat takes (at least a week's worth)
- ID tag attached to your cat's collar
- Leash and harness
- Blankets
- Collapsible food and water bowls
- Photo of your cat in case you become separated

Other supplies

_____

_____

_____

It's also a good idea to keep printed copies of your cat's vet records and any license and registration documents you have from your city/county.

IMPORTANT INFORMATION:

My vet's contact information

_____

_____

_____

If you had to evacuate your home, where would you go with your cat?

_____

_____

_____

Names and phone numbers for pet-friendly hotels in those areas

_____

_____

_____

MEDICAL RECORDS

Our cats rely on us to keep them safe and healthy, which can be challenging because cats can't actually tell us how they are feeling! In fact, some cats are very stoic and will attempt to hide illnesses. With that in mind, it's important for kitties to be getting regular vet visits for vaccinations and to monitor their health. Keeping copies of your cat's vet records—especially proof of vaccinations—somewhere easily accessible is important, especially in the case of an emergency.

Vet Name: _____

Vet Phone: _____

Vet Address: _____

Next Appointment: _____

Due For _____

Closest Emergency Vet: _____

Phone: _____

Address: _____

Keeping baseline health information is helpful. What is normal for your cat?

Weight: _____

What food does your cat eat? _____

How often does your cat eat? _____

How much does your cat eat? _____

Any known health conditions:

_____

_____

_____

Medications or supplements your cat takes monthly:

_____

_____

_____

Medication or supplements your cat takes daily:

_____

_____

_____

Flea and tick prevention:

_____

_____

_____

WHEN SICK

Writing down the details of your cat's symptoms when they aren't feeling well can be very helpful in making sure they get the best veterinary care as quickly as possible. Bringing your written notes to the appointment can help you clearly and effectively communicate what's going on with your cat and help your vet reach the right diagnosis. It's scary and sad when our cats are sick because they can't tell us exactly what's wrong, but the more information we can gather, the more it will help get them feeling better sooner.

Symptom Tracker:

_____

_____

_____

Pain:

_____

_____

_____

Eating:

_____

_____

_____

Drinking:

_____

_____

_____

Peeing:

_____

_____

_____

Pooping:

_____

_____

_____

Other Symptoms:

_____

_____

_____

If you have a medically fragile or senior cat, I recommend keeping an active-symptom chart like this, including daily eating habits, in a notebook that you can update daily or weekly. By keeping a close focus on your cat's health, you may be able to notice when symptoms become more serious. It's also a good idea to keep physical proof of your cat's vaccinations printed out in a folder or folded and stapled into this activity book, so they are easy to access.

THE MANY PHASES OF YOUR CAT

Naptime is important for cats. Cats can sleep up to twenty hours a day! Where does your cat enjoy sleeping? What positions does your cat like to sleep in? For this section, pay attention to your cat's napping habits, and doodle your cat's naptime positions. Something I love about cats is how confident they are. Try to channel that confidence when you draw—don't worry about being a "good" artist, just focus on having fun and documenting your cat's positions.

Napping position one

Napping position two

Napping position three

Napping position four

Napping position five

Napping position six

RULES!

Is your cat in charge of the house, or do you have a lot of rules? Some people don't let their cats into the bedroom or on the kitchen counter. Having rules for your cat's behavior isn't a bad thing! Living with a cat companion should be mutually rewarding for both of you, and if there are things that bother you, it's okay to ask your cat not to do them.

Do you have rules for your cat? _____

What are your cat's rules?

_____

_____

_____

Having rules is not the same thing as being stern or mean. When teaching your cat to follow rules around the house, it's important to be gentle and use positive reinforcement methodologies. Instead of scolding or punishing your cat for doing something you don't like, reward your cat for the behaviors you do like. A great way to do this is to reward your cat anytime they do something you like, and to reward them for doing behaviors that are incompatible with ones you don't like. For example, if you know your cat likes to jump on the counter while you are cooking dinner, give them a treat, puzzle, or toy in another part of the home before you start to cook.

How have you trained your cat in the past?

_____

_____

_____

Are there behaviors your cat does that bother you? List a behavior you struggle with (like jumping on the counter), and then a positive alternate behavior you could offer to your cat instead.

"Problem": _____

Alternate behavior:

_____

_____

"Problem": _____

Alternate behavior:

_____

_____

"Problem": _____

Alternate behavior:

_____

_____

"Problem": _____

Alternate behavior:

_____

_____

THAT'S THE SPOT!

Just as some people love to be hugged, and others of us prefer a little more personal space, cats have preferences around how and when they are touched. In particular, many cats have preferences about where on their body they get pets. For example, many cats prefer to be petted and scratched at the base of their ears, and under their chin as opposed to on top of their heads.

Does your cat have petting preferences? On the model cat on the following page, choose colors to represent loves, likes, tolerates, and dislikes. Color in the boxes associated with each of those feelings to create a key.

 Loves

Likes

Tolerates

Dislikes

Now, on the model cat below, take the colors you chose above and color in the corresponding areas on your cat. Not only can this be a fun exercise to help you think critically about how your cat does or doesn't like to be touched, it can also be helpful to share with pet sitters, visitors, and even your cat's vet!

MAKE YOUR CAT INTERNET FAMOUS

Does your cat have their own social media account yet? Cats rule the internet when it comes to popularity. It seems like everyone loves a cat photo and building online "friendships" with the cats they follow. If you have a cat that enjoys taking pictures, putting them online can be a fun opportunity to save memories and document your life together. It's also a great way to meet like-minded cat lovers and their cats, and even build friendships. Some cats have even turned being social media influencers into a career, monetizing posts, partnering with brands, and doing product reviews.

What social media platforms is your cat already on?

_____

_____

Social media is always growing, changing and evolving. Having success with your cat online has to come from a genuine place. If you and your cat aren't having fun with what you are creating and posting, that will be obvious, and you aren't likely to gain followers. Don't forget to utilize hashtags, including things like the city where you and your cat live, the breed of cat you have, if your cat is a rescue, cats of [social media platform], etc. Hashtags are an easy way to find other cat accounts, and to allow other cat accounts and cat lovers to find you.

Don't ever do anything that's risky or that makes your cat uncomfortable just for a view. Have fun creating and managing online profiles for your cat, but don't get too preoccupied with it. Be sure to spend quality time with your cat, not just doing things for the purpose of documenting it.

Make your cat a social media profile and add other cat accounts as friends! Use the section below to keep notes about how many followers your cat has, what other cats you add as friends, what you like and don't like about engaging with other cats online, etc.

_____

_____

_____

_____

_____

BEST IN SHOW

Whether your cat has won ribbons at shows, or your cat is "Best in Show" in your heart, all cats are amazing. What makes your cat special? For this next activity, create your own cat show! Consider making an award or ribbon for your cat to put on the fridge or post on social media. Is your cat the best at napping? Cuddling? Making you laugh? Cheering you up after a bad day? No matter what your cat's talents are, take time to celebrate them!

What does your cat do best?

_____

_____

What does your cat love most?

_____

_____

What is cutest about your cat?

_____

_____

In what ways is your cat smart?

_____

_____

In what ways is your cat clever?

_____

_____

What is the funniest thing your cat does?

_____

_____

What is the weirdest thing your cat does?

_____

_____

Is there something your cat does that is different from other cats you know?

_____

_____

BEST IN SHOW
AWARD

_____

IS BEST IN SHOW FOR

_____

_____

GROOMING GOALS/CHALLENGE

Keeping your cat well-groomed is important for maintaining their overall health. Although most cats will naturally groom themselves, it's important to groom them yourself as well. Grooming is also a great way to spend quality time bonding with your cat. Depending on your cat's coat type, you may need to groom more frequently than once a week, but all cats, even short-hairs, should get regular weekly grooming. Long-coated cats may need it on a daily basis to keep their fur clean and free of mats. Keeping your cat's coat free from matting promotes healthier skin and prevents sores from developing. In addition to regular brushing of your cat's fur, you'll want to check their ears to make sure they are clean and healthy and consider brushing their teeth and trimming their claws (if that's your preference and your cat is exclusively indoors).

Grooming is a great opportunity to get hands-on with your cat and gently feel for any new lumps, bumps, or changes in their skin so that you can bring them to the attention of your vet. Building a regular grooming routine is an important part of taking care of your cat. Keep notes on how far you make it through your grooming routine weekly, and if there are any things you want to remember, positive or negative, like finding a mat in their fur, or them being excited to participate in grooming.

Month 1

Week 1	Week 2
Date:	Date:
Brushing:	Brushing:
Nails:	Nails:
Other:	Other:
Notes:	Notes:
Week 3	Week 4
Date:	Date:
Brushing:	Brushing:
Nails:	Nails:
Other:	Other:
Notes:	Notes:

Month 2

Week 1	Week 2
Date:	Date:
Brushing:	Brushing:
Nails:	Nails:
Other:	Other:
Notes:	Notes:
Week 3	Week 4
Date:	Date:
Brushing:	Brushing:
Nails:	Nails:
Other:	Other:
Notes:	Notes:

Month 3

Week 1	Week 2
Date:	Date:
Brushing:	Brushing:
Nails:	Nails:
Other:	Other:
Notes:	Notes:

Week 3	Week 4
Date:	Date:
Brushing:	Brushing:
Nails:	Nails:
Other:	Other:
Notes:	Notes:

Month 4

Week 1	Week 2
Date:	Date:
Brushing:	Brushing:
Nails:	Nails:
Other:	Other:
Notes:	Notes:

Week 3	Week 4
Date:	Date:
Brushing:	Brushing:
Nails:	Nails:
Other:	Other:
Notes:	Notes:

CRAFTS

MAKE A MEME

Cats are the stars of the internet, and they are the stars of memes! If you're anything like me, you probably have a whole collection of go-to cat memes to make you laugh. For this activity, you're going to create your own cat meme, starring...your cat! Memes tend to be funniest and most shareable when they feature a small amount of text that is relatable and timely. Many memes reference something going on in the news or pop culture, but they can also be more personal.

For this activity, you can use a photo manipulation program on your computer or phone, or you can take a picture of your cat, print it out, and use blank self-stick address labels (or just little pieces of paper and a glue stick) to make a meme on the page! Once you make your meme, you can post it on your (or your cat's) social media!

Use this space to brainstorm ideas for a meme featuring your cat:

_____

_____

_____

_____

_____

Paste a picture of your cat meme below and use stickers or paper and glue to add in the text of your meme:

CATIO DESIGN

It's important for cats to live indoors for their safety and the safety of local wildlife. If you have a cat who is interested in the outdoors, a great way to give them access to the outside world in a safe and controlled way is to build a catio for them. Catios have grown in popularity in recent years.

Catios can be as simple as a small area outside your window, or a large enclosure that takes up a large portion of your backyard. Safe construction of the catio is important to make sure that your cat can't escape and that other animals in your neighborhood can't get into it. Many professional contractors will work with you to create the catio of your cat's dreams and do the building for you. Or, if you're handy with tools, you can build one yourself. If you rent your home, be sure to get permission from your landlord before installing a catio.

Do you have a catio for your cat?

_____

_____

Do you think your cat would like a catio?

_____

_____

Use the space below to sketch out your ideas for an ideal catio setup for your cat.

CAT SCRATCH ART

Does your cat have an inner artistic side? For this activity, you're going to give your cat the chance to create some real art that you can frame, hang on your refrigerator, or give to a pet sitter, friend, or family member who also loves your cat.

Supplies Needed:

- Scratch art paper—which can be ordered online or found at most craft stores
- Cat treats, toys, or catnip

Scratch art pages have a soft, nontoxic outer layer that can be scratched away, revealing colors underneath. These pages are designed for kids to play with, but they actually also work really well for creative kitties!

Step 1: Get your scratch paper out at a time when your cat is awake and eager to engage with you.

Step 2: Put some treats, catnip, or toys onto the scratch page to encourage your cat to engage. Catnip in particular will often encourage cats to scratch or knead at the paper underneath, creating an interesting artistic pattern.

Step 3: When your cat scratches at the scratch art paper, praise and continue to give them treats.

Step 4: When you are satisfied with the amount of scratch drawing your cat has done, praise them and marvel at their artistic creation!

PAW PRINT CREATIONS

For cats who are comfortable having their paws handled, paw painting is an enjoyable activity you can do together to create art to hang in your home or gift to friends and family!

Supplies Needed:

- Nontoxic washable paint or ink pads—ink pads designed for babies and pets can be ordered online or purchased at a craft store
- Paper—you can do this craft right on the pages of this book, but you will want extra paper (it should be easy to frame and hang)
- Damp washcloth to wipe your cat's paws after painting
- Markers, paint, or other craft supplies of choice for decorating the paw prints

Paw painting can be messy, so this is a great activity to do in your kitchen or bathroom, where it's easy to wipe up floors. You can also lay out some old magazines or newspapers or an old sheet as a drop cloth to protect your floor from paint and ink.

Instructions:

Step 1: Put some of the nontoxic paint onto a paper plate or open up the nontoxic ink pad. Gently place your cat's paw into the paint or ink pad.

Step 2: Place your cat's paw on the page and carefully lift up while praising your cat.

Step 3: Gently wipe your cat's paw with the washcloth, praise, and give your cat treats.

Step 4: Repeat the above steps, making sure to praise and treat your cat after each paw print.

Step 5: When the paint or ink has dried, go back with paint, markers, etc.

Now it's time to decorate! Turn the prints of your cat's paw print in different directions and see what kinds of shapes or images you see. Teddy bears, flowers, and turkeys are all popular things to make with your cat's paw prints. How many things can you make using your cat's paw print?

CAT BOX TOWER

Climbing is a natural activity for cats. Being able to climb and get height is not only fun for cats, it is also comforting. Cats enjoy climbing when they are playing, but also, when they are nervous or uncertain about a situation, getting height can help them feel more confident. Giving your cat regular access to furniture, cat trees, and other safe climbing opportunities is important for them.

To add some climbing activity for your cat, you can use extra boxes to build a cat tower! Start collecting sturdy boxes that come with deliveries and other purchases. When you have a decent number of boxes, make a plan to put them together to build a cat tower! You can cut crawl holes, doors, and windows into the boxes and attach them together using heavy tape for stability.

Use the space below to draw ideas for a cat box tower.

You can make your cat tower look any way you want. You can make it look like a house, or a skyscraper, or a castle. To get some ideas, search online for different types of architecture. You can also use nontoxic cat-safe paint to decorate the box tower.

What design did you pick for the box tower?

_____

_____

What did your cat think of the box tower?

_____

_____

Post a picture of the completed box tower:

NO-SEW CAT BEDS

If your kitty is always looking for a cozy place to nap, these no-sew beds are a quick and easy craft to make! With these beds, you can create the perfect nap spot for your kitty in every room of your home. They are even easy to wash!

Supplies Needed:

- 🐾 Two one-square-yard pieces of fleece in any pattern or color of your choice; you can even use different fleece patterns for each side to make it reversible
- 🐾 Batting or stuffing to put inside the bed

Instructions:

Step 1: Start with the two fleece pieces, each a yard square, and cut them down to whatever size you want your cat bed to be. Leave two to three inches extra on all four sides.

Step 2: Cut slits around the perimeter of both pieces of fleece, so that the outside of each piece is fringed. Make each slit a couple of inches long.

Step 3: Lay the fleece pieces together with the "back" sides facing each other so the outsides of both pieces are facing out.

Step 4: Tie the strips from the two pieces of fleece together. Double-knot the pieces together, then leave half of one side of the rectangle open to leave room for the stuffing.

Step 5: Add in the stuffing, as generously as you want, depending on your cat's preferences for how fluffy the bed is. Remember, as your cat sleeps on the bed, the stuffing will break down a little, so it's a good idea to start with some extra stuffing.

Step 6: Finish by double-knotting the remaining strips to close up the bed.

Step 7: Fluff the bed to make sure the stuffing is evenly distributed, and then give it to your kitty to enjoy!

Extras: This bed is simple and inexpensive to make, making it easy to have a variety of seasonally themed beds available. Fabric stores often get festive fleeces in stock, so you can make festive holiday beds for your kitten and then trade the beds out for each season.

Looking for ways to give back to less fortunate cats? On your own, or with a group of friends, you can get a lot of fleeces and make a large batch of these no-sew beds to donate to a cat shelter or rescue group in your local area. This would be fun to do during the winter holiday season, or any time of year.

Note: Be sure to contact rescue groups or shelters in advance to make sure this is a donation that would be welcome and useful to them at this time.

SNUFFLE MAT! NOT JUST FOR DOGS!

Although most snuffle mats are marketed for dogs, they offer a foraging activity that cats enjoy as well! Cats have a much better sense of smell than we do, and having the chance to forage and explore is a fun and enriching activity for cats. Snuffle mats can also be used to make mealtime more fun for your cat (if they eat kibble).

Snuffle mat exploration is a self-directed activity that cats of all ages can enjoy. You can purchase commercially available snuffle mats online or at pet stores, or you can make your own!

Make a DIY snuffle mat:

Supplies:

- Two yards of fleece—you can purchase whatever is on sale or pick a color scheme that matches your household decor or your cat's personality; you can even combine multiple colors, textures, and widths of fleece to provide additional texture to your mat

- A plastic sink drainer mat or plastic craft mesh—you can usually find either of these very inexpensively at dollar stores. We will use this for the base of our kitty snuffle mat

Instructions:

Step 1: Cut the fleece into strips half an inch to an inch wide by four to eight inches in length.

Step 2: Double-knot your fleece strips through each hole in the base, going all the way down the length of the mat row by row.

Step 3: Go back and double-knot more fleece strips (it helps to use a different color so you can better see where you are going) through the holes again, on the diagonal, making an X shape with the two strips of fleece at each hole.

Step 4: Once you have tied the fleece through the mat, you will have one side that's flat (that will be the bottom), and the other side with the knots and the ends of the fleece strips—this is the side that will be fun for your cat to forage in.

Now it's time to play! Take some dry kibble or dry kitty treats and sprinkle them into the snuffle mat. Show your cat the snuffle mat and encourage them to start searching—most cats take to this activity right away.

Note: Be sure to supervise your cat while they are playing with the snuffle mat. Most cats are happy just to sniff and snack, or maybe bat at the fleece strips as they search for food or treats, but occasionally cats will try to chew on the fleece strips, which could be a safety hazard. If you notice your cat is trying to chew or eat the snuffle mat, take it away immediately.

DINNER IS SERVED!

Want to give your cat the opportunity to experience fine dining? You can design a custom placemat for your kitty!

Supplies:

- Art supplies of your choosing: markers, colored pencils, paint, glitter, etc.
- Legal-sized pieces of white (or other colored) paper
- Stickers, old magazines, etc. (collage materials)
- Laminator, or your local office supply or coffee shop where you can take your placemats to be laminated

Use the next page to doodle design ideas for your cat's placemats. Don't be afraid to use your imagination!

Some ideas: Write your cat's name in a fancy script; place arrows for where the food and/or water bowls should go. Doodle your cat's favorite things, like toys or food, or make the placemat look like a fancy restaurant menu—you can even come up with a cute or funny name for the restaurant. You can make placemats for different seasons and holidays and then trade them out.

Don't forget to decorate both sides of the placemat to make it reversible, so you can give your cat two placemats in one! When you come up with ideas you like, recreate the design on the actual placemat, laminate, and give it to your cat to enjoy!

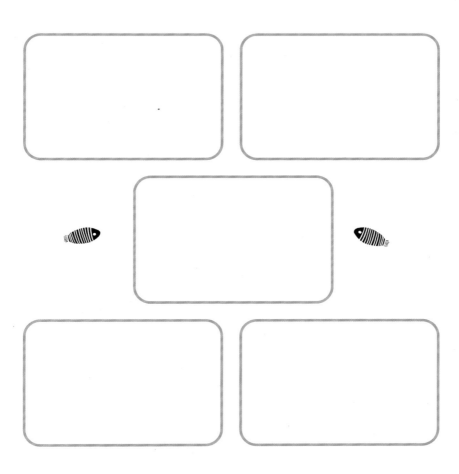

CAT FLUFF ART!

If you have a cat, especially a long-haired cat, chances are you have more than a little bit of cat fur around your house. Keeping your cat regularly groomed is really important for your cat's overall health, and to keep their skin and coat in good condition. If you find yourself with a lot of fur after grooming, you don't have to just throw out all the fur—you can do cat-fur-inspired crafts.

KNITTING

Fur that has been brushed off your cat (not matted fur that has been cut) can be spun into yarn the same way sheep or alpaca wool is! You can make cat yarn by going old-school and learning how to card and spin the fluff into yarn yourself at home. Alternatively, there are companies you can send the clean cat fur to that will return it to you as yarn that you can then craft with. This spun yarn can be knitted or crocheted into anything from scarves and hats to a special keepsake blanket.

DONATE TO WILDLIFE

Does your cat enjoy spending time watching birds out the window? If cat-fur crafts aren't quite your style, you can donate your cat's clean fur to wildlife in your yard or in a local park. If you put out clean cat fur, birds will pick up the discarded fluff and use it to make nests. Who knows, you might even inspire the birds to stick around your yard and nest in your trees, providing unlimited entertainment for your cat watching from the window.

ORNAMENTS

Using your cat's fur to make Christmas ornaments and keepsakes is a simple craft. Most craft stores carry clear plastic bulb ornaments. These ornaments are also available in glass, but plastic is a safer option for Christmas trees in homes with cats. These ornaments are designed to be painted inside, but when the top comes off, instead of painting, you can add clean cat fur!

Once the fur is inside, you can use paint pens or other craft supplies to decorate the outside of the bulb or ornament with your cat's name or doodles of your cat. This ornament makes a special keepsake to have on your Christmas tree for years to come or can make a great gift for friends and family who also love your cat.

PHOTO PROPS!

Cats and the internet seem to go together! Taking photos with your cat is a fun way to capture special moments together, but the selfies you take don't have to be serious. For this activity, you'll be making some silly photo props and having an impromptu photo shoot of your cat, or with your cat.

Think about cat-related memes or jokes on the internet and how you could reenact them. Draw a cartoon laptop or fish, or you could try more traditional photo props, like mustaches, monocles, sunglasses, bows, or top hats! Use your imagination while brainstorming and creating photo props for your cat.

Supplies

- Dowels, skewers, or chopsticks for holding up the photo props
- Tape
- Construction paper or cardstock
- Markers, paint, and/or colored pencils to decorate your props with
- Scissors

Instructions

Step 1: On the construction paper or cardstock (cardstock will hold up best), sketch or trace the outlines of different shapes you want to use as props.

Step 2: Cut out each of the photo props that you draw.

Step 3: Add any colors, details, or decorations you want to include.

Step 4: Use the tape to attach the dowel, skewer, or chopstick to the prop.

Next, show the props to your cat. Have treats ready and reward your cat for being near the props. If your cat isn't concerned about being near the props, then slowly hold them up to your cat and give the cat a treat. If your cat seems nervous or uncomfortable, back up and start rewarding them for the props being present at a distance. Once your cat is comfortable with the props being held near, you're ready for photo shoots!

> **Note**: Be sure to supervise your cat when they are near the photo props to ensure they don't try to chew on them.

In the space below, doodle ideas you have for props, or paste in photos you took of/with your cat using the props:

SILHOUETTE ART

Want to add a cat to all your crafts? Silhouettes are an easy way to catify any craft project and give things a classic cameo-like touch. For silhouette crafting, you'll want to take a picture of your cat standing sideways in profile or find a picture of a cat standing in profile online.

Instructions:

Step 1: Print the photo of your cat or the cat picture you find online.

Step 2: Take your photo and a blank piece of paper and trace the shape of the cat onto the page. Tracing paper works best, if you have it, but plain computer paper or notebook paper also works. Especially if you're using computer or notebook paper, it's helpful to hold the picture and paper up to your window or a computer screen to create a DIY light box and make it easier to trace.

Step 3: Once you have an outline of the cat's silhouette, you need to cut it out for use as a stencil. If you want to use the stencil repeatedly, you can trace your silhouette onto a piece of cardstock or soft plastic which will last longer (but may be more difficult to use on rounded objects).

Step 4: Place your cat's silhouette on the object you want to add it to, like a pumpkin, a vase, a shirt, or even a decorative piece of wood or plate. Trace around your cat's silhouette using a pencil or marker, depending on the surface, and remove the stencil.

Step 5: Depending on the surface you're putting your cat silhouette on, now it's time to carve out the silhouette (if you're working on a pumpkin), or use paints, markers, or other craft supplies to fill in the cat silhouette. You can aim for realistic designs, or get creative!

Fun options: use fantasy colors to paint your cat's silhouette, add stars, sprinkle glitter, draw your cat's favorite things into the silhouette, or add their name.

SEASONAL ACTIVITIES

CAT HOLIDAYS

JANUARY

January 14: National Dress Up Your Pet Day

FEBRUARY

Cat Dental Health Month

Spay/Neuter Awareness Month

National Cat Health Month

Pet Theft Awareness Day

APRIL

April 23: National Pet Parent Day

Last Friday in April:
 Hairball Awareness Day

April 30: Adopt a Shelter Pet Day

National Pet First Aid Awareness Month

MAY

National Pet Month

JUNE

Adopt a Cat Month

June 4: Hug Your Cat Day

Friday after Father's Day:
 Take Your Pet to Work Day

National Pet Preparedness Month

JULY

July 10: National Kitten Day

July 15: National Pet Fire Safety Day

AUGUST

August 8: International Cat Day

Immunization Awareness Month

SEPTEMBER

National Disaster Preparedness Month

Second Sunday in September:
  National Pet Memorial Day

OCTOBER

National Animal Safety and
Protection Month

October 4: World Animal Day

Third Week of October:
  National Veterinary Technician Week

October 27: National Black Cat Day

October 29: National Cat Day

NOVEMBER

National Pet Cancer Awareness Month

Senior Pet Month/National Adopt a
  Senior Pet Month

First week of November:
  Animal Shelter Appreciation Week

November 13: World Kindness Day

BIRTHDAY PARTY FOR KITTY!

Your cat is one of your best friends, so it's only natural you want to spoil them on their special day! Some of us know the exact day when our cats were born, and some of us have no idea because they were found or rescued. The good news is that cats are always ready to party with us, so you can pick a date anyway and select it as your cat's birthday! You can also pick a date close to when you suspect your cat was likely born, or celebrate your kitty's "gotcha" day—the day they came home with you—as their birthday.

On what day do you celebrate your cat's birthday?

_____

Make a list of your cat's favorite things:

_____

_____

_____

Read back over your list and circle any things your cat loves that you might be able to incorporate into their birthday.

INVITATIONS

Do you have a social kitty? If your cat has people they enjoy spending time with, consider inviting them to your cat's birthday party! You can make or purchase invitations. Of course, you can just send a text message, but actually sending an invitation makes things feel more fun. If you aren't feeling crafty, kid's birthday invitations are a cute and inexpensive option. You may even be able to find cat-themed party invitations, paper plates, etc., at your local dollar store. If you have a shy kitty, you can skip this step and keep the party to just you and your cat!

Make a list of your cat's favorite people:

_____

_____

_____

_____

_____

MENU

There are many commercially available cat birthday cakes and cupcakes that can be ordered. There are even cat cake box mixes you can purchase to bake at home! Don't forget to have snacks available for yourself or any guests you invite. If you're feeling creative, you can even make cat-themed snacks, like cutting sandwiches into cat shapes and using pretzels for whiskers or putting cat faces on any of the other foods you are serving.

Snack options:

_____

_____

_____

_____

PRESENTS:

Don't forget to spoil your cat with their favorite treats and toys for their birthday!

Insert a picture of your cat's birthday party celebration here:

KITTY EASTER EGG HUNT

An Easter egg hunt is a classic way to celebrate during the Easter season. This Easter, you can throw your cat their very own Easter egg hunt! For this activity, you will want to get an assortment of plastic eggs and treats that your cat is excited about.

How to Play:

Step 1: Fill the plastic eggs with your cat's treats—one treat in each egg.

Step 2: While your cat is in another room, hide the plastic eggs in places that your cat can safely reach. In the space below, keep track of where you hide the eggs, so you can make sure your cat finds them all.

Step 3: Once all the eggs are hidden, bring your kitty back into the room where the eggs are hidden and encourage them to start searching!

Hint: To introduce your cat to the idea of the egg hunt, it can help to start with one egg not at all hidden but right out in the open. Show the egg to your cat and let them figure out there are treats inside. From there, most cats will be ready to search!

Where did you hide eggs?	What eggs did your cat find first?

Be sure to always supervise your cat while they are having an Easter egg hunt. The plastic eggs can easily shatter if they are chewed on, which could become a choking hazard.

GARDENING WITH YOUR CAT

A fun way to spend quality time with your cat any time of year is to do some indoor gardening together! Cats are naturally inquisitive, so it's important to make sure that any plants you bring into your home are pet-safe. The ASPCA's online Poison Control website is a wonderful resource to keep bookmarked in your phone for double-checking that any houseplant you are looking at buying is safe for your cat to be around.

You don't need a lot of space to have a cat-friendly window garden, just be sure to select planters or pots that are heavy enough that your cat won't easily be able to knock them over. You can select pet-safe decorative plants or go for edible plants that you and your cat can grow, tend, and snack on together! Green beans, zucchini, peas, and carrots are some veggies that are safe to share with cats. Another option is to get cat grass, or catnip, starts or seeds to plant for your cat to enjoy. These plants can make a great addition to a window seat or other area you want to encourage your cat to spend more time in.

Where did you put your cat-friendly garden?

_____

_____

_____

What was your cat's reaction to the addition of plants?

_____

_____

_____

What plants did you select for your cat garden?

_____

_____

_____

Keep track of how your garden grows, and if you bought edible plants, report back on what your cat thought of what you grew:

_____

_____

_____

CAT HALLOWEEN COSTUMES

Do you love to get dressed up for Halloween? Although it's a staple of the holiday for most people, getting dressed up can be stressful for our cats. Although there are a lot of Halloween costumes on the market for cats, most cats don't naturally enjoy getting dressed up. The key to helping your cat enjoy getting dressed up for Halloween is planning ahead.

If you pick a Halloween costume for your cat on Halloween and just put the costume on them, it's unlikely to be a very fun or successful evening for your cat, and instead will be very stressful. Instead, it's important to come up with costume ideas well in advance, so you can introduce your cat to the costume intentionally and slowly. When looking at pre-made costumes or making your own, be sure to keep your cat's comfort in mind.

Cat Costume Advice:

- Find or make a costume that your cat can fit comfortably into. Focus on making sure the costume is not restrictive of your cat's legs.
- Be wary of any outfits with hats or headpieces. Although some cats are fine with these accessories, many find them uncomfortable and stressful.
- Plan your cat's costume as far in advance as possible, so you have time to make sure they are comfortable with the costume before Halloween.

INTRODUCING YOUR CAT TO THE COSTUME

Step 1: First, put the costume out on the floor or on furniture where your cat is comfortable, and let them sniff and explore the costume.

Step 2: Praise and give your cat treats for sniffing or engaging with the costume.

Step 3: When your cat is comfortable engaging with the costume, it's time to start putting it on. Gently put the costume on your cat while giving treats and lots of praise.

By pairing wearing the costume for very short sessions with treats and praise, you can help your cat develop positive appreciations of the costume. You can also invite your cat to play with toys while wearing their costume. If at any point your cat seems stressed or uncomfortable with the costume, remove it immediately.

Brainstorm Halloween costume ideas for your cat here:

What costume did you pick for your cat?

_____

CAT HALLOWEEN PUMPKIN

Cats and Halloween just go together! This year, consider making the pumpkin you carve or paint cat-themed. You can try to draw your cat onto the pumpkin or go with a more generic cat design. There are templates you can find online to print and trace onto your pumpkin, or you can draw your own!

In the space below, sketch out your design for your cat-themed pumpkin:

GRATITUDE

This is an activity that's fun to do around Thanksgiving, but I like to center gratitude all through the year, not just for one day in November. For many of us, our cats are the highlight of our lives; they are our constant companions, and bright joy to our days. For this activity, you are going to be reflecting on your relationship with your cat. What are your favorite things to do together? In what ways does your cat make your life better?

Write one thing every week this year that you are thankful for about your cat and your relationship:

1.	19.	37.
2.	20.	38.
3.	21.	39.
4.	22.	40.
5.	23.	41.
6.	24.	42.
7.	25.	43.
8.	26.	44.
9.	27.	45.
10.	28.	46.
11.	29.	47.
12.	30.	48.
13.	31.	49.
14.	32.	50.

15.	33.	51.
16.	34.	52.
17.	35.	
18.	36.	

Looking back at your year together, what are your favorite memories? Feel free to paste in pictures from your year, or write about what you and your cat have done, times your cat's company meant the most to you, etc.

_____

_____

_____

What are some things you think your cat is grateful for?

_____

_____

ADVENT CALENDAR

Do you enjoy sharing the fun of the Christmas season with your cat? Advent calendars are a fun way to ring in the season and give ourselves a small treat every day of December as we wait for the big day. Although the most popular advent calendars are for human children and contain little candies or small toys, increasingly advent calendars are becoming popular for everyone, including adults and even cats!

Cat advent calendars can be purchased at some specialty grocery stores and at pet supply stores, or you can make your own! If you have a picky kitty and you want to give your cat a custom advent calendar, an easy way to create this is to purchase a plain empty advent calendar at a craft store. These come in all kinds of designs, from simple boxes to more elaborate designs. If you purchase one of these empty advent calendars, you can then find or purchase twenty-four small treats or toys for your cat to open and unbox each December day leading up to Christmas. I've been doing advent calendars with my cat for several years now, and my cat is obsessed with his. Within a couple of days, he is into the routine and looking forward to his nightly treat after dinner!

Has your cat ever had an advent calendar?

_____

_____

Below, make a list of the kinds of treats you want to collect to fill your cat's advent calendar with!

1.

2.

3.

4.

5.

6.

7.

8.

9.

10.

11.

12.

13.

14.

15.

16.

17.

18.

19.

20.

21.

22.

23.

24.

What did your cat think of opening their advent calendar each day?

_____

_____

_____

Did your cat start to anticipate the daily ritual of opening a box?

_____

_____

_____

What other Christmas festivities do you and your cat enjoy? What new ones do you
want to start?

_____

_____

_____

EXPLORE THE WORLD

WORK AT HOME WITH KITTY

During the COVID-19 pandemic, many of us have adjusted our lives to spend more time at home...with our cats! Most of our cats have enjoyed all the extra opportunities to spend time with us, and for people who work office jobs that have gone remote, every day has become take your cat to work day!

Has your cat ever joined you on a video meeting?

_____

How does your cat respond to you being at work (while at home)?

_____

Do your coworkers' cats also come to meetings?

_____

What is the funniest thing your cat has ever done while you are working from home?

_____

_____

Next time you find yourself stressed during the day, take a break after your next meeting and play with your cat. Not only will it be fun for your cat, but it will be some much-needed stress relief for you!

KITTY SAFARI

For indoor cats, your home is literally your cat's entire world. Keeping this in mind, it's clear why it is so important to make sure that your cat has access to enriching toys, scratching surfaces, and climbing structures. The goal should always be to find ways to enrich your cat's day and living environment. Even though your cat knows your home well, our cats are always exploring.

Spend some time observing your cat and what they are doing. What places in your home does your cat like to explore?

_____

_____

As part of their explorations, many cats like to find and claim "treasures." Sometimes these are cat toys, and sometimes they are things that don't belong to your cat. Keep a list of the interesting treasures that your cat collects around your home, like shoelaces, hair ties, bugs, paper balls, etc.

_____

_____

PLAN A CAT STAYCATION

Do you hate the thought of traveling because it means leaving your cat behind with a cat sitter? You aren't alone! Traveling without your cat sometimes can't be avoided, and, honestly, some of our cats really enjoy time with a qualified pet sitter. That said, if you're feeling the need for some time off, but also don't want to be without your cat, think about scheduling a staycation with your kitty. You can pick a long staycation if you have the time, or just a weekend or long weekend. The focus of your staycation should be spending quality time with your cat, doing the things that the two of you most enjoy doing together.

Pick dates for your staycation:

_____

What will you and your cat do to spend quality time together, such as playing, sleeping in, movie days, etc.?

_____

_____

Are there any cat-friendly people foods that your cat especially enjoys getting to sample that you might want to add to your staycation menu plan?

_____

_____

How did the staycation go?

_____

_____

_____

What was your favorite part?

_____

_____

_____

What do you think was your cat's favorite part?

_____

_____

_____

NIGHT IN WITH KITTY

After a long hard day, do you look forward to spending some quality time with your cat? For many of us, getting home to see our cats is a highlight of the day. Although cats might have a reputation for aloofness, they are deeply bonded to their people and enjoy spending quality time with their families.

Sometimes life gets in the way of us spending as much time as we might want to with our cats, so for this activity, we're going to make quality time with our cat the priority. If you get invited to meet up with friends, just respond, "Sorry I can't, I have plans." It's not a lie; you do have plans, with your cat! Plan an evening when you have time to focus on your cat and won't get distracted by answering emails or doing chores. Try to focus on doing the things that you and your cat enjoy best!

What are your favorite things to do with your cat when you get home?

_____

_____

If you could pick a perfect way to spend an evening at home with your cat, what would you do?

_____

_____

_____

What games would you play?

_____

_____

_____

If you have a cuddly cat, consider spending time on the couch cuddling up and watching a movie. You can even pick a cat-themed movie! What did you watch?

_____

_____

_____

VACATION WITH KITTY

Do you have an adventurous cat? If your cat enjoys exploring the world, traveling can be a fun way to spend time with them. Many people travel in RVs or vans (#VanLife anyone?) with their feline companions. Additionally, increasingly, hotels are becoming more welcoming to cats! In addition, private rentals are often open to renting to cats and their people. My cat Thing enjoys regularly traveling to a beach cottage, where he is happy to relax and then get cozy with us when we get back from a day on the sand.

HOTEL TIPS

If you're going to be staying in a hotel with your cat, it's important to make sure the hotel is cat-friendly when booking your room. When you arrive at the hotel, before letting your cat explore, be sure to closely inspect the whole room to ensure there isn't anywhere your cat could get stuck or lost, such as into a bed frame, or a gap behind cabinetry. If there are aspects of the room you don't feel good about, it can be safest to keep your cat confined to the hotel room's bathroom and let them out into the hotel room just on leash for safety. Never leave your cat unattended in a hotel room.

Have you ever traveled with your cat?

_____

_____

_____

Where did you go?

How did your cat react?

Where did you stay?

How did you get there?

What was it like to travel with your cat?

Paste in a picture of your vacation with your cat:

FANTASY VACATION

Is there someplace you have always dreamed of traveling with your cat? Is it a real place? Is traveling there reasonable? Some dream vacations might be possible, while others might be more fantastical for a variety of reasons, including your cat's temperament, whether the place would be safe for your cat, whether they allow cats, and of course financial considerations. Realistically, we can't always take the vacation of our dreams, but it's still fun to dream about it!

If you could travel anywhere with your cat, where would you go? (This can be a real place or imagined.)

_____

_____

_____

_____

Why do you want to travel there?

_____

_____

_____

How would you get there?

_____

_____

_____

What would you and your cat do here?

_____

_____

_____

Where would you stay?

_____

_____

_____

How long would your vacation be?

_____

_____

_____

What would you bring for your cat?

_____

_____

_____

What souvenir would your cat want to bring home?

_____

_____

_____

What would your cat like best about this trip?

_____

_____

_____

CRATE TRAIN YOUR CAT

Is it a battle to get your cat into a crate or carrier every time you need to go to the vet? It doesn't have to be this way! Being comfortable and happy going into their crate is an important skill for all cats to have, because you never know when you'll need to transport your cat. In a carrier is the safest way for your cat to travel by car for visiting the vet, moving, or other travel. In addition, if you ever need to fly with your cat, you'll need to have them in a carrier. The goal of crate training your cat is for your cat to develop a positive association to the crate, and not see it as something negative, or something to avoid.

Supplies Needed:

- Cat crate or carrier
- Treats that your cat enjoys

Instructions:

Step 1: First we want to help our cat to have a positive relationship and association to the crate. Leave the crate out with the door open for your cat to explore. If you see them sniffing or exploring near or in the crate, praise them and give treats.

Step 2: Put treats and/or their food into the crate and praise them for going in to eat. Keep the crate door open—our goal right now is just to help your cat make positive associations with the crate.

Step 3: After several practice sessions when your cat is happily going into the crate on their own to get treats/food, praise them and close the door of the crate for a moment, praise them, give a treat through the crate (if your crate has window/air holes you can fit treats through), and immediately let them out.

Step 4: Over time, slowly build up the amount of time your cat is in the crate with the door closed, including slowly introducing lifting the crate, and eventually, taking the crate outside and into your car. It can be helpful to give your cat longer-lasting treats, like a LickiMat covered in wet cat food, while they are in the crate to continue to help them make positive associations.

Does your cat like their crate? _____

Use the section below to make notes on how crate training with your cat has gone.

_____

_____

_____

_____

_____

_____

_____

_____

_____

_____

_____

AIR TRAVEL TIPS

One of my favorite cat memories will always be when my partner and I were moving cross-country to New York City with our two cats. I had never flown with a cat before, but thankfully, with a little bit of preparation, the flight went smoothly!

You never know when you might need to fly with your cat, so it's good to be prepared. If you're looking to book a flight with your cat, be sure to look at the specific requirements and restrictions from your airline of choice and from the destination. Some airlines require cats to be in specific carriers, and some states or countries have specific requirements for what kind of documents you need for your cat to enter.

HARNESS ON!

When you fly with a cat, you will need to remove your cat from their carrier to pass through security. For your cat's safety, it's a good idea to have them wearing a securely fitted harness with a leash attached to help you keep hold of them to get safely through security.

UPDATED ID

Before flying with your cat, make sure that they have been microchipped and that their microchip information has been updated. You should also make sure your cat is wearing an identification tag with updated information.

SEDATIVES

Many people want to get sedatives for their cats before a flight. If you are interested in sedatives, be sure to talk with your veterinarian in advance to find out if they are right for your cat. If possible, plan to start having these conversations in advance, so you can do a home trial with any medication before your flight to learn how your cat will respond. We thought we were going to want to give our cats some medications to help them relax on the flight, but we learned during the trial that it didn't help our particular cats relax—in fact, they had the opposite reaction! Glad we found that out before we were on the airplane!

PACKING

If you're going to be flying with your cat, it's important to fly with everything your cat will need for the flight, and for immediately after the flight. When I flew with my cats, I brought a foldable portable litter box in our luggage and Ziplocs of cat litter along with food, so that the cats could be set up with everything they needed as soon as we got off the flight.

Have you ever flown with your cat?

_____

If yes, what was the experience like?

_____

_____

_____

_____

LEASH TRAINING YOUR CAT

The thought of taking your cat for a walk might sound silly, but a lot of cats enjoy getting the chance to explore outside. For their safety, and the safety of wildlife, cats should always live inside, but if you want to give your cat some outdoor space and time, teaching them to enjoy going for a leash walk is a safe way to do that, especially for bold kitties who are curious about doors.

Supplies Needed:

- Four- or six-foot lightweight leash
- Cat harness appropriately sized for your cat
- Cat treats

Instructions:

When starting to leash train your cat, you want to start inside your home, in a place where your cat is comfortable. This is where we want to introduce the harness and leash to our cats to make the experience as stress-free and enjoyable as possible.

Step 1: Show your cat the harness and leash. Praise and reward your cat for sniffing or expressing any interest in them.

Step 2: Put the harness onto your cat, praise, and give your cat treats or play with a toy, and then immediately remove the harness.

Step 3: Start to leave the harness on for slightly longer periods of time, and engage your cat in play with toys, or with treats, while wearing the harness.

Step 4: When your cat is comfortably wearing the harness while playing, it's time to start working on walking. Do not pull your cat with the leash—instead, use treats and/or toys to encourage them to walk in a specific direction in your house while you hold the leash.

Step 5: When your cat is comfortably following treats and toys on leash in your house, it's time to start venturing outside. Make sure that the harness is properly fitted to your cat, and select a time and location outside that is quiet, like your backyard, or your front yard at a time when there isn't a lot of activity happening. Allow your cat to explore at their own pace and level of comfort, while offering them treats and praise for being outside. Keep your outing short and successful!

The more confident your cat gets with exploring outside, the more you can start to vary the locations you visit, and even have your cat walk a little bit in your neighborhood. Be sure to keep a good hold on the leash and watch your cat's body language for any sign of fear or discomfort. If you see another animal approaching, for your cat's safety, pick your cat up. If your cat seems uncomfortable, pick them up, offer lots of praise and treats, bring them back inside, and try again another day. Keep all walks short and fun; the goal isn't to see how long a walk you can take your cat on, but rather to keep the outings fun and enjoyable.

How did your cat react to being introduced to the leash and harness?

_____

_____

_____

Keep track of the places (front yard, back yard, down the block, etc.) you go with your cat and your cat's reactions.

Place:

_____

Reaction:

_____

_____

_____

Place:

_____

Reaction:

_____

_____

_____

Place:

_____

Reaction:

_____

_____

_____

Place:

_____

Reaction:

_____

_____

_____

Place:

_____

Reaction:

_____

_____

_____

STROLLER WALK

If you have a cat who is curious about the outside world but not so sure about a leash walk (or if you are nervous about taking your cat out on a leash), another option is to stroller train your cat. There are a variety of strollers designed specifically for cats. These strollers look like strollers for human babies, but instead of a baby seat, they have a soft zipped compartment where your cat can be safe while looking out at the world.

Step 1: If you get a stroller for your cat, it's important to introduce them to the stroller at their own pace. Bring the stroller inside your house and let your cat explore getting in and out of it. To encourage your cat to explore the stroller, you can put some of their toys or treats in it.

Step 2: When your cat is comfortably getting into the stroller, you can close the soft crate portion for a moment, praise your cat, and then open it again. Each time, you can slowly increase the amount of time that you keep the stroller closed for.

Step 3: Over a few sessions, when your cat is comfortable being zipped into the stroller, you can gently start to roll it in your house. It can help to provide your cat with treats and toys inside the stroller to continue to reinforce that it is a fun and positive space.

Step 4: When your cat is comfortable being rolled around in the stroller inside, it's time to bring them outside for a stroller walk. Pick a time of day that is quiet in your neighborhood, so as not to overwhelm them. Keep your first walk short and fun, and don't forget to talk to your cat while they are out on a stroller walk.

Does your cat enjoy riding in a stroller?

_____

If you take your cat out on stroller walks, keep track of the places you go and your cat's reactions!

Place:

_____

Reaction:

_____

_____

_____

Place:

_____

Reaction:

_____

_____

_____

Place:

_____

Reaction:

_____

_____

_____

Place:

_____

Reaction:

_____

_____

_____

Place:

_____

Reaction:

_____

_____

_____

SHOPPING SPREE!

This is an activity that is best for social kitties who are used to leash walking (see page 140) and who are comfortable going places. This activity is a way to spoil your cat, or a chance for you and your cat to give back to those less fortunate by donating everything your cat picks to a local rescue group or shelter.

Bring your cat on leash to a pet supply store and plan to purchase everything your cat touches or explores. It's completely okay (and a good idea) to set a budget and limit on how much you are going to spend before you come. It's also best to pick a time to visit the pet supply store when they are likely to be quiet to give your cat the chance to "shop" in peace and quiet.

For extra fun, you can bring a friend to video your cat picking out items in the store and upload it to your or your cat's social media pages!

BEFORE YOU GO

What kinds of toys or treats do you think your cat is going to pick out?

_____

_____

_____

What is your budget?

_____

AFTER YOUR VISIT

How was your cat's shopping spree?

_____

_____

_____

How did your cat react to being in the store?

_____

_____

_____

Were people surprised to see a cat shopping?

_____

_____

_____

What did your cat pick out to buy at the store?

_____

_____

_____

Did anything your cat picked surprise you?

_____

_____

_____

Did you have to say "no" to anything your cat seemed interested in?

_____

_____

_____

If you decided to donate what your cat picked out, where did you donate?

_____

Did you stick to your budget?

_____

MUSIC TIME!

Some cats take off to another room in the house when you turn the music on. On the other hand, some cats seem to actually like the music their people listen to.

What does your cat think of your musical preferences?

_____

How does your cat react when you play music?

_____

Do a little experiment and play different types of music. Does your cat react differently from genre to genre? Record your cat's reactions to different genres of music below:

Rock   Hip-Hop

_____   _____

Classical   Techno

_____   _____

Reggae   Jazz

_____   _____

Country   Other

_____   _____

What type of music do you think was your cat's favorite?

_____

AT-HOME TREASURE HUNT

If you're looking to add some enrichment to your cat's day, a great way to do that is to take treats, dry food, or toys your cat is excited about and hide them around your home. Start in areas that aren't too hidden at first so that your cat can be successful in their search. The better your cat gets at the game, the more complicated hiding spots you can pick for the treats!

This activity provides great mental stimulation as cats puzzle out where the "treasure might be." It also encourages your cat to use their sense of smell, which is very enriching for cats.

What are some of your favorite places to hide treats for your cat?

_____

_____

_____

_____

_____

_____

Create a treasure hunt for your cat by hiding toys or treats around your house. In the space below, keep track of where you hide treats for your cat, and then which ones your cat finds first!

Hiding locations:

_____

_____

_____

How long did it take for your cat to find all the treasures?

_____

What did your cat think of the treasure hunt?

_____

_____

_____

GAMES AND CHALLENGES

BUBBLE ART

Most cats enjoy the opportunity to chase things. Bubbles are a fun and inexpensive way to provide some chase and enrichment fun for your cat inside. You can purchase cat-specific bubbles, including some that are flavored like catnip, chicken, or other cat favorites. If you don't have any cat-specific bubbles, you can also use nontoxic children's bubbles—just be sure to read the ingredients before playing with your cat to ensure that there are no toxic ingredients for cats in that brand of bubbles. Chasing bubbles can get a little bit messy, so this is a game best played in the kitchen or another area of your home that can be easily wiped down after you and your cat are done playing.

To start playing, get your cat's attention and blow a few bubbles, not at your cat, but in a direction where your cat can see them. How does your cat react to the bubbles?

_____

_____

_____

Next, blow some bubbles onto the page and trace the outline of the bubbles:

VIDEO GAME CAT!

Does your cat ever try to bat your phone or tablet out of your hands? As we spend an increased amount of time on our phones, our cats often become interested in what we're doing. Some cats take those moments to try to get onto our laps and between us and our electronics, other cats are more interested in the electronics and what we are doing.

If you have a cat who is always curious about your phone, it can be fun to give your cat the opportunity to have some screen time of their own! There are a variety of video games for cats that have been developed for use on smartphones or tablets. These games generally involve moving objects or animals on the screen for cats to "catch."

It's important to note that video games are not a great option for every cat. Laser pointers can cause stress and frustration for cats because they are unable to actually "catch" the moving light which can leave them feeling dissatisfied and frustrated. The same can also be the case with kitty video games. That said, some cats really enjoy and seek out opportunities to play "their" games. If you decide to try kitty video games, be sure to closely monitor your cat to make sure they aren't stressed by the activity.

GAME DAY ONE

What game did your cat play?

_____

What is your cat supposed to do to win the game?

_____

In the space below, record your cat's reaction to the game:

_____

_____

_____

GAME DAY TWO

What game did your cat play?

_____

What is your cat supposed to do to win the game?

_____

In the space below, record your cat's reaction to the game:

_____

_____

_____

GAME DAY THREE

What game did your cat play?

_____

What is your cat supposed to do to win the game?

_____

In the space below, record your cat's reaction to the game:

_____

_____

_____

GAME DAY FOUR

What game did your cat play?

_____

What is your cat supposed to do to win the game?

_____

In the space below, record your cat's reaction to the game:

_____

_____

_____

BOX THEME PARK

Most of us have seen our cats enjoy getting the chance to play in boxes regardless of whether we want them in those boxes! For this activity, we are going to give cats the chance to play in boxes to their heart's content. As you purchase items or get deliveries in the mail, try to put aside and save good-sized boxes in a closet or other out-of-the-way area. When you have a decent number of boxes collected, it's time to create a theme park for your cat!

For this activity, you can use scissors to cut holes in the boxes for doors, windows, and pass-throughs. You can use packing tape to attach boxes together to create larger boxes, box tunnels, and box towers! Be sure to make sure that the structures that you create with the boxes are stable enough not to fall over when your cat starts to play in them. For extra fun, put some of your cat's favorite toys into and around the boxes to inspire even more ways to play.

In the space below, draw your design ideas for the box amusement park you want to build for your cat:

After you finish building your kitty amusement park, draw or take a picture of the theme park you've created for your cat and include it below:

What did your cat think of the kitty amusement park?

_____

_____

_____

What part of the structure did your cat enjoy best?

_____

_____

_____

How long did this activity hold your cat's attention?

_____

_____

_____

GO FISHING!

Cats naturally enjoy using their paws to explore and bat at things in an attempt to catch them. To support your cat's natural fishing instinct, you can create enrichment games and activities for them. Your "fishing" games can include water, if your cat is interested in playing with water, or can be dry "fishing" games—whatever your cat will enjoy most!

Supplies Needed:

- Bowl
- Cat toys
- Cat treats

Tip: If you have a cat who enjoys playing with water, you can even get cat toys that "swim" and are specifically designed for cats to use in water.

Instructions:

Step 1: Take a large bowl and fill it partly full of water.

Step 2: Drop cat toys, balls, and other plastic or rubber toys into the water. Some toys will float while others will sink, which only adds to the game for your cat. Alternatively, in a shallower bowl, you can drop a few treats into the water.

Step 3: Show your cat the fishing bowl and let them explore the fishing game.

How did your cat react to the fishing bowl game?

_____

_____

_____

Did your cat catch their toys in the water?

_____

List what toys your cat caught first:

_____

_____

_____

If you have a cat who isn't interested in playing with water, you can use the bowl without water in it to play. This game will still elicit some of the same fishing-like behavior from your cat.

SHELL GAME

Is your cat ready to gamble? For this game, your cat will find hidden treats under a paper cup! Using their nose, your cat will determine which of three cups has a treat hidden under it.

Supplies Needed:

- Three paper cups
- Cat treats

Instructions:

Step 1: Start with one cup and a smelly treat your cat is excited about. Let your cat watch you put the treat under one of the cups.

Step 2: Let your cat explore the cup and when they sniff or paw at the cup, praise and lift the cup so they can get the treat.

Step 3: Repeat this several times until your cat is confidently knocking over the paper cup with the treat underneath it. If you want, you can introduce a verbal cue like "gamble" or "search."

Step 4: Next, bring in another cup, but only put a treat under one. Don't "shuffle" or move the cups around yet. When your cat knocks over the right cup, give lots of praise and lift the cup so they can get the treat.

If your cat paws at the empty cup, no problem, just lift it up and show them there isn't anything there. Then, lift the cup with the treat under it to show your cat, but don't let them get the treat. Put the cup back down and let them search. When they get the right cup, give lots of praise.

Step 5: When your cat is constantly alerting to the right cup by using their nose to figure out which cup has the treat, you can make things more complicated by adding in a third cup (but only putting a treat under one). You can also start to shuffle the cups after putting the treat under one to make it more challenging for your cat to find.

As your cat gets better at the game, be sure to start shifting which cup has the treat on it—so, for example, make sure it's not always the middle cup with the treat.

What did your cat think of the shell game?

_____

_____

How long did it take your cat to catch on?

_____

_____

Is your cat ready for Vegas?

_____

_____

AGILITY COURSE!

Although agility is technically a dog sport where dogs jump, climb over obstacles, weave between poles, and fly through tunnels, at-home versions of agility can be a lot of fun for your cat. If you have an active cat who loves to explore, creating an at-home agility course might be the perfect activity for you and your cat!

Safety Note:

The idea behind creating the agility course is to provide a creative outlet for your cats. It's not about trying to see how high your cat can jump. Safety should always be the top priority—avoid asking your cat to jump on slick flooring like hardwoods or tile, and instead set up an agility course for them on an area rug or other carpeted area of your home to make sure your cat has traction as they are moving.

You can purchase at-home agility courses for dogs, but you can also get creative and make obstacles yourself!

- You can make jumps out of a broomstick propped onto books or boxes.
- Use an ottoman for your cat to jump up onto in the middle of the course.
- Create a tunnel by opening both ends of boxes.

Look around your house and get creative to see what you can use to create an obstacle course for your cat to explore. Once you have it built, you can lure your cat through with toys or treats!

In the space below, sketch the obstacle course you are going to build for your cat:

SPLASH GAMES!

Although cats have a reputation for not liking water, many cats enjoy having the opportunity to play in or around water. Many enjoy having access to running water (my own cat Thing has actually learned how to turn on the kitchen sink when he's bored with waiting for birds to come visit his bird feeder). If you have a cat who enjoys the chance to play in water, it's possible to provide your cat with access to splash games you can create for them, in addition to "go fishing" on page 163!

BATHTUB PLAYTIME!

If you have a cat who enjoys drinking from or playing with running water, you can turn on your bathtub faucet at a slow trickle, put some of your cat's toys into the bathtub (choose waterproof toys that aren't plush), and encourage them to play.

FOUNTAINS

Thera are a number of commercially available cat water fountains that you can purchase to have in addition to or in replacement of one of your cat's water bowls. These recirculating fountains give your cat continual access to running water without also wasting water by leaving the water on.

Does your cat enjoy playing in the water?

BIRD FEEDER

Is your cat curious about the world outside? A fun way to provide enrichment to your indoor kitty's day is to install a bird feeder outside your window. This can be mounted in your yard or one that actually attaches to the window (this is the feeder my cat Thing prefers). A bird feeder that uses suction cups to attach to your window will bring birds right up to where your cat easily sees them without risking the safety of the birds.

Before putting up the bird feeder, think about what window will work best for the feeder. Try to avoid putting the feeder in or near a window that has breakable collectibles or plants on the windowsill, to avoid those getting broken by your cat as they enthusiastically watch the birds. Windows near a cat tree or comfortable furniture—or where you can put a window cat bed or other comfortable place for your cat to rest while watching the birds—are ideal to keep your cat comfortable and entertained.

How did your cat respond to the bird feeder?

_____

_____

What kind of birds came to your feeder?

_____

_____

BALL PIT PLAYTIME

If you're looking for a way to spoil your kitty with a new enrichment activity or game, you can invest in a kid's ball pit for your cat to play with! These ball pits can be purchased in the toy section of most big box stores or online. You can buy the balls on their own and then put them in your bathtub, or you can purchase a kit that includes a popup tent or pen for the balls.

Don't force your cat into the ball pit—instead, let your cat explore it on their own. If your cat seems nervous, start with just a few balls in the pit at first, and add more during later play sessions. To encourage your cat to play in the ball pit, you can add some of their favorite toys in with the balls, or even sprinkle catnip or a few treats in with the balls.

What did your cat think of the ball pit?

_____

_____

_____

_____

_____

_____

_____

BURIED TREASURE

Cats are naturally inquisitive, and some of their favorite enrichment games are those which give them the opportunity to explore. This pirate game is an opportunity for cats to get creative as they search for hidden treats and toys.

Supplies Needed:

- Old clean magazines and newspapers
- Bathtub or empty baby pool
- Treats or toys your cat is excited about

Instructions:

Step 1: Take the old magazines and newspapers and crumple up the pages into little balls.

Step 2: When you have a large number of paper balls completed, put them into your empty bathtub or an empty plastic baby pool.

Step 3: Add some toys and/or treats into the crumpled-up paper balls.

Step 4: Show your cat the treasure area and let your cat explore!

Note: Be sure to always supervise your cat while they are playing the pirate dig game to make sure they don't start trying to chew on or eat the balled-up newspapers!

What things did you hide amongst the paper for your cat to find?

_____

_____

_____

What did your cat think of the pirate search activity?

_____

_____

_____

CUPCAKE TIN PUZZLE

Keeping your cat mentally enriched is just as important as making sure they are getting enough physical activity. Just as puzzles are a great way to stretch your brain, the same is true for cats! There are a number of commercially available puzzles for cats (as well as puzzles for small dogs which can be used by our cats). Having a few puzzles on hand can be a great way to keep your cat occupied and decrease boredom, but you don't have to spend money to give your cat interesting puzzles to play with!

Supplies Needed:

- Twelve tennis balls
- A cupcake baking pan
- Treats your cat is excited about

Note: For small cats and kittens, you can get a mini cupcake tin and mini tennis balls to make the puzzle more appropriately sized.

Instructions:

Step 1: Put treats into a few of the components of a cupcake pan.

Step 2: Tennis balls fit perfectly into the holes of a standard cupcake tin, so after you put treats into some of the cupcake compartments, put tennis balls on top of all the compartments.

Step 3: Show your cat the cupcake pan and encourage your cat to search for the "hidden" treats.

How fast did your cat find the treats?

_____

_____

_____

What did your cat think of the puzzle?

_____

_____

_____

This is a puzzle your cat can play repeatedly—just switch up what compartments of the cupcake tin you put the treats into!

SODA BOTTLE PUZZLE

For this puzzle activity, your cat will use their paws to flip empty soda bottles (which are hanging from a dowel) to access treats you have put inside. This puzzle is a great way to reuse extra plastic soda bottles and is a fun enrichment activity that will keep your cat mentally stimulated!

As with any other puzzle, you should always supervise your cat while they are playing with this toy.

Supplies Needed:

- Wooden dowel long enough to suspend between chair legs with bottles threaded on
- Three one-liter plastic bottles
- Scissors
- Treats or dry food

Instructions:

Step 1: Use your scissors to cut holes slightly larger than the diameter of your dowel through the tops of the soda bottles, below the necks.

Step 2: Thread the dowel through the holes in the bottles.

Step 3: Take small treats or some of your cat's dry food and put them into the bottles.

Step 4: Position the dowel between the legs of chairs to keep it stable.

If your cat enjoys this soda puzzle, for a more advanced version, you can build a stand to hold the soda bottle dowel. This will make the bottles more stable and allow you to put the game anywhere in your home for your cat to play with.

How quickly did your cat solve the puzzle?

_____

_____

_____

What did your cat think of the puzzle?

_____

_____

_____

SHOE BOX PUZZLE

This puzzle is designed to give your cat the opportunity to channel their inner hunting instincts without leaving your living room!

Supplies:

- 🐾 Cardboard shoe box
- 🐾 Newspaper
- 🐾 Cat treats and/or toys

Instructions:

Step 1: Take an empty shoe box and cut a few holes in the lid and in the sides. The holes should be big enough that your cat can fit their paw into them.

Step 2: Ball up some old newspaper into balls and put them into the shoe box.

Step 3: Sprinkle some treats and/or toys into the shoe box and then put the lid on.

Step 4: Show your cat the shoe box and let them have fun "fishing" with their paws into the shoe box puzzle to get the treats and toys out!

PAPER BAG GAMES

Even if you enjoy buying your cat a lot of fancy toys to play with, cats have a reputation of being simple creatures when it comes to their play habits. For many cats, paper bags, like those from the grocery store, are a favorite toy. For these activities, you will need paper bags—small or large ones will work—and some dry food or treats your cat likes.

INTERACTIVE FEEDER

A simple way to make your cat's mealtime more exciting is to engage them in foraging activities at mealtime. To do this, take a clean paper bag and put some dry food or treats into the bag. Your cat will be able to "hunt" and pounce on the bag to find their food. For an added challenge, you can bring out multiple paper bags and put food into all of them, or just some of them. You can also twist the bag closed, so your cat will need to figure out how to open the paper bag to access their food or treats.

PUZZLE TIME

You can also turn paper bags into a puzzle by cutting or ripping holes in the bag. Then, drop some kibble or treats into the bag, fold it closed, and leave it standing for your cat to explore. Your cat can then reach into the bag to access their treats or food.

Note: Be sure to only allow your cat to play in paper bags. Plastic bags are dangerous for cats to play with, as they can suffocate in them or bite off and ingest parts of the plastic.

What did your cat think of the paper bag games?

_____

_____

_____

What activity is your cat's favorite?

_____

_____

_____

HOW MANY THINGS CAN YOU DO WITH A BOX?

One of the great things about training your cat and doing enrichment games together is that you don't need a lot of equipment or special supplies. Quite literally, you can train your cat and play enrichment games with supplies that you have around the house.

Some of my favorite training props are boxes—not only do they make great easy enrichment puzzles, they can be used in a variety of other ways. Small boxes can be turned on their side and you can make cat hurdles (remember to keep jump heights low for safety and have your cat jump on carpet or other supportive footing) for your cat to jump over. You can put two boxes parallel to each other and ask your cat to go between the boxes, or to jump from one box to the next box.

For this activity, we're going to see how many things you and your cat can figure out to do with a box! Most of us have a lot of different-sized boxes around from deliveries. The best box for this activity will be a sturdy one that can hold the weight of your cat and that is large enough for your cat to get into. Have some treats handy and see how many things you and your cat can figure out to do with a box! Examples include front feet in, all feet in, two paws on, all paws on, find hidden treats, jump over box, pull toys out of box, etc.

How many things can your cat do with a box?

THIRTY DAYS OF ENRICHMENT CHALLENGE

Have you found some activities that you and your cat enjoy? Just like us, cats can become bored, which can have a direct impact on their physical and mental health. Between family and work commitments, it's easy for life to get in the way of spending quality time with your cat, but even just a few minutes a day can make a huge difference in the quality of your cat's life. One of my favorite ways to build confidence and my relationship with my cat is to develop fun training challenges to inspire me to train or play daily with my cat.

TAKE THE CHALLENGE

Are you and your cat ready for a challenge? For the next thirty days, can you and your cat find something fun to do together each day? Get creative! Try a new game, play a favorite game, feed your cat's meals in enrichment toys instead of a bowl. The most important aspect of the challenge is to make sure that you and your cat are having fun together.

Keep track of the activities you and your cat do each day on the following page.

1.

2.

3.

4.

5.

6.

7.

8.

9.

10.

11.

12.

13.

14.

15.

16.

17.

18.

19.

20.

21.

22.

23.

24.

25.

27.

28.

29.

30.

TRICKS

TRICK CATS

Does your cat know any tricks? Many cats enjoy learning to do different behaviors on cue. Trick training can provide cats with a great outlet for their energy. Trick training provides cats with physical and mental enrichment. Trick training is also a wonderful way to spend quality time with your cat.

How many behaviors does your cat know on cue?

_____

_____

Are there tricks you want to teach your cat?

_____

_____

If you want to start trick training with your cat, there are a few different behaviors included in this book. If you're looking for other trick training advice, my book *Tricks in the City*, while designed for teaching dogs tricks, can be adapted for teaching tricks to your cat! If you and your cat enjoy trick training, you can earn titles together! Don't let the name fool you, the organization DMWYD (Do More with Your Dog) allows animals of all species to earn titles from Novice to Grand Champion!

HIDE & SEEK

Hide and seek isn't just a fun game for kids, it's an enjoyable game that you and your cat can play together! Hide and seek can be played in even the smallest of apartments. This is a game that can get your cat moving and is very mentally stimulating. To play the game, you'll want to leave your cat in one area of your home and sneak out of the room to a different area.

When you first start playing, don't hide too well, just begin by going into another room or area of your home and start calling your cat. When your cat finds you, give them lots of praise and treats. The more experienced with the game your cat gets, the more difficult you can make your hiding place. Try crouching behind a piece of furniture or behind the back of an opened door. Just make sure wherever you hide, it is somewhere that your cat can easily find and get to (i.e., avoid hiding in a closed closet).

If at any point your cat is taking a long time to find you or seems lost, you can always call your cat again to give your cat a little bit of extra help to get to you.

Record your hide and seek adventures with your cat below! Where did you hide? Did your cat find you? How long did it take for your cat to find you?

_____

_____

_____

COME WHEN CALLED

Teaching your cat to come when called might sound impossible, but it's something that cats can have fun learning. Teaching your cat to come when you call isn't just a fun trick, it has the potential to be lifesaving if your cat were to ever dart out a door, or they were missing somewhere in your house.

The goal of teaching your cat to come is that the activity should always be fun, and we want to reward our cats for choosing to be near us. It's essential to never punish or scold your cat for coming, even if they are slow.

Supplies Needed

- Treats your cat is excited about
- Toys your cat is excited about

Instructions

Step 1: Start with a high-value treat your cat is excited about and treat your cat every time they look at you. This is all about building value for your cat in being near and engaged with you.

Step 2: When playing with your cat, as they move toward you (when you are sure they are moving toward you) praise and offer treats or engage them with a toy.

Step 3: Now, when your cat is moving toward you and you are sure they are going to continue coming, introduce the verbal cue you want to use such as "come," "here," or "recall," and give them lots of treats and praise when they get near you.

Step 4: Continue practicing your cat's "come" cue, making sure to always reward them when they approach you.

Don't be afraid to take this activity slow. The most important thing when teaching your cat to come is not to introduce the verbal cue too early, or you risk weakening your cat's understanding of it.

GOTCHA! RECALL GAME

Once your cat knows how to come when called (page 187), a fun activity can be to practice this skill by playing recall games with your cat. These are games designed to continue helping your cat to build value with coming to you when called—they also are a lot of fun!

This fun recall game will get you and your cat up and moving! With a toy that your cat is excited about, get your cat's attention and then move across the room as quickly as possible. You can call "kitty, kitty, kitty" or another excited phrase that is *not* your recall cue or your cat's name. The goal of the game is for your cat to choose to chase after you, but you don't want to risk confusing the meaning of your recall cue by using it if you aren't sure your cat will follow you. When you run away from your cat and they turn to follow you, praise and engage them with the toy as soon as they get to you.

Did your cat follow you right away?

_____

_____

What did your cat think of the gotcha game?

_____

_____

PICK A HAND, ANY HAND

This classic magic trick of which hand holds the prize can be played with your cat. For this activity, your cat will be using their sense of smell to determine which hand you have a hidden treat in! Although people generally think of dogs when it comes to sense of smell, our cat friends also have an incredible sense of smell and can tell a lot more about the world by what it smells like.

Supplies Needed:

🐾   Treats your cat likes

Instructions:

Step 1: Put a cat treat in one of your hands and show it to your cat without letting your cat get it.

Step 2: Close your fist around the treat and close your other fist as well.

Step 3: Hold both of your hands out to your cat.

Step 4: When your cat paws or noses at the hand with the treat inside, open your hand and give them the treat with lots of praise!

If your cat paws or nuzzles at the "wrong" hand without the treat, open your hand to show your cat there isn't anything in that hand. Show your cat the treat in your other hand and close it again, without letting them get the treat, and start again. When your cat selects the correct hand, give lots of praise and let them have the treat!

When your cat starts to understand this game, you can start to move the treat between your hands back and forth, so your cat isn't sure by sight what hand the treat is in. Hold both hands out to your cat to sniff, and then select a hand. When your cat gets it right, immediately give lots of treats!

This is a fun "magic" trick to show off with your friends or recording videos for your social media!

What did your cat think of the pick-a-hand magic trick?

_____

_____

_____

_____

_____

_____

TEACH YOUR CAT HIGH FIVE

Do you wish your cat knew more tricks? Trick training is a great way to spend quality time bonding with your cat and teaching them skills. High five is a relatively easy starter trick to teach your cat.

Supplies Needed:

   Treats your cat is excited about

Instructions

Step 1: When your cat is awake and engaged with you, get a treat and put it in one of your hands and hold it up to your cat.

Step 2: Your cat will likely start to nuzzle or sniff at your hand—ignore this.

Step 3: When your cat reaches up with a paw to your hand, praise and give your cat the treat from inside your hand.

Step 4: Repeat until your cat is constantly pawing at your hand with the treat inside, then hold up your hand without a treat in it. When your cat paws at your hand, praise and give a treat!

Step 5: Now it's time to introduce a verbal cue of your choice—like "shake," "high five," "gimme some," etc.

SPIN!

Is your cat ready to dance? Spin is a relatively easy trick to teach cats and is sure to impress your friends at your next home dance party.

Supplies Needed:

- Treats your cat is excited about

Instructions:

Step 1: When your cat is standing in front of you, get treats in both of your hands.

Step 2: Show your cat the treats in your hand and, with their nose on the treat, lure them in a wide circle. When your cat comes back to facing you, praise and give the treat.

Step 3: After a few repetitions, when you are sure your cat is going to follow the treat to spin, you can start to add in the verbal cue of your choice while your cat is spinning. Common cues include "spin," "twirl," and "spiral."

Step 4: When you are teaching this trick, be sure to practice luring your cat to spin both clockwise and counterclockwise.

Step 5: When your cat is constantly spinning by following the treat, you can start to phase out the lure and transition to just a smaller physical cue. To do this, have treats next to you but not in your hand and ask your cat to spin, making a small circle gesture with your hand (a smaller version of the larger lure you started with).

PLATFORM TRAINING

With platform training, we are going to teach our cats to go to a target mark, a raised platform, or a bed on cue. Platform training is useful if you and your cat ever want to put together a trick routine, but it's also a very practical way to reduce conflict in the home with your cat and be able to ask your cat to go to a specific location on cue.

Supplies Needed:

- 🐾 Platform or target of some kind; it can be a raised table like a KLIMB platform (available online), a yoga mat, a towel, or a cat bed
- 🐾 Treats

Instructions:

Step 1: Take a treat your cat is excited about and, when you are a couple of feet from your platform, get your cat's attention with the treat and get excited and animated as you quickly guide them to the platform. When your cat follows you and gets up onto the platform, drop the treat and praise.

Step 2: After a couple of repetitions, when you are confident your cat is going to follow you to the platform, you can start to add a verbal cue as you are in motion with your cat following you, and then gently toss the treat onto the platform for your cat. Cues can be anything you want. Popular options include "place," "spot," "mark," and "target."

Step 3: Next, put the treat on the platform and give your verbal cue while moving with your cat toward the platform, but without luring your cat with a treat. When your cat goes to the platform and gets the treat, offer lots of praise and treats.

Step 4: Next, you can start putting treats on the platform for your cat, giving the verbal cue, but not walking all the way to the platform with your cat. When your cat gets onto the platform praise as they are eating the treat and move in and give more treats.

Step 5: After a few practice sessions, you can start to phase out having the treat on the platform, and just bring a treat to your cat when they get to the platform or toss a treat to your cat on the platform.

Platform skills are a great force-free way to move your cat around the house without having to pick them up and physically move them. Just be sure to keep this activity fun and rewarding by rewarding your cat for going to their place on cue, and not immediately picking them up and starting to do something they might find stressful or unpleasant, like grooming or going into a carrier (if those things aren't enjoyable for your cat).

TRAINING CHALLENGE

Patience and consistency are the essential qualities for training with any animal, and especially with cats. Training sessions should be kept short and fun—just a few minutes each day, or a couple of times a day, is far more effective than trying to drill behaviors over and over again in a single session. Instead, make training a regular part of how you and your cat spend quality time together. To build this habit, set a challenge of doing some form of training with your cat every day for thirty days!

In the space below, write what activity you and your cat are working on each day:

1.	16.
2.	17.
3.	18.
4.	19.
5.	20.
6.	21.
7.	22.
8.	23.
9.	24.
10.	25.
11.	26.
12.	27.
13.	28.
14.	29.
15.	30.

HUMAN ACTIVITIES

GIVING BACK

Most of our cats are lucky enough to have pretty much everything they could want or need, but a lot of cats in our communities aren't so lucky. These cats might be in shelters and rescues, homeless and being fed or cared for by volunteers, cared for by families who have fallen on hard times and are struggling financially, or living with people who are experiencing homelessness or who are struggling to pay their bills and keep kibble in the bowl!

As we focus on pampering our kitties, it's nice to think about ways that we can give back to other cats, cats who are struggling in our local community. Most areas have community shelters or rescue groups, and increasingly, people are organizing pet food banks! Pet food banks are available for people who are financially struggling or who are experiencing homelessness and can provide them with dry and canned cat food and other necessities. Pet food banks also often organize regular no-cost vaccines, spay/neuter, and veterinary clinics so that cats can get appropriate medical care regardless of their family's ability to pay.

Search online for organizations in your local area for groups or organizations providing support for homeless cats or people experiencing homelessness with their cats, and find out what kind of support they need. Organizations often need volunteers, as well as financial support and donations of cat food, cat treats, toys, blankets, cat litter, and other cat supplies.

Organizations in your local area:

_____

_____

_____

What are some ways you can support the organization with your time or resources?

_____

_____

_____

What are ways you can inspire friends, colleagues, family, etc., to support organizations helping needy cats in your local area?

_____

_____

_____

CATS WITH JOBS!

Cats are some of our oldest companions. It is believed that humans and cats began living together and forming a close relationship around 7500 BC! Most of our cats are beloved pets and household companions, but some cats also have jobs! Do you think your cat would like to work?

Therapy Cats: A therapy cat has a natural ability that is then honed through training to support and visit people in nursing homes, hospitals, and similar settings. Therapy cats bring comfort to people who are ill or isolated. Therapy cats need to be comfortable around diverse groups of people and not show fear or aggression toward people or animals. Various organizations will test and certify cats and help coordinate visits to local care facilities and hospitals. If you have a very social cat who you think would make a good therapy cat, and if you are interested in volunteering as a therapy cat team, contact your local Humane Society for information about groups in your local area.

Military Cats: Cats might not have been enlisted in the military the way dogs have been and are, but cats have been an active part of the military, often as part of rodent control! Cats have been companions of sailors, and welcomed into the barracks not just for their companionship, but also because of their ability to keep rodent populations low.

Blood Donors: Just as, after surgery or a serious injury, a person might need a blood transfusion, cats also sometimes need to receive blood while in a veterinary hospital. The cats who donate that blood are not forced; they are confident social cats who go on a regular basis. If you are interested in learning more about the need for cat blood donors in your local area, a good place to start is with large veterinary hospitals. Many of them have animal blood donor volunteer programs.

Performing Cats: Every time you see a cat on television or in a movie, that cat is a trained actor! The same is true when cats appear in commercials or print advertisements. Cats who act in television and film greatly enjoy the work they do. These cats enjoy training and learning new skills so that they can appear as though they are "acting" in the scene that they are appearing in. If you have a cat who has mastered a lot of training and is very confident and social, you might have a future movie star on your hands! Cat trainers in your local area, or local talent agencies, will be able to give you tips about how to start auditioning for roles.

VISIT A CAT SHOW

Did you know that there are cat shows? The Cat Fanciers Association (CFA) has been around since the early 1900s. Attending a cat show in your local area is a great way to connect with other cat lovers, and to learn about different breeds of cats. If you're interested in getting involved, many cat shows have a Household Pet division, which means you and your cat could even participate. If you're interested in learning more, CFA.org has a wealth of information about finding local shows in your area to visit or participate in, and can help you learn more about the rules and regulations for how to get involved!

Look for information about the next cat show in your local area and make plans to attend!

Next cat show: _____

Date: _____

Location: _____

What was it like at the cat show?

_____

_____

_____

Do you think you would ever want to get involved with showing cats?

_____

_____

_____

What was your favorite of the cats you saw?

_____

_____

_____

Print and glue in pictures or draw pictures of some of the cats you saw.

CAT SPOTTING!

Are you someone who sees cats everywhere you go? Cat spotting is a fun activity you can play while traveling, or just walking around your neighborhood. If you pay attention, you'll see a lot of cats, cats in windows, cats on fences, cats that live or work in shops. In the space below, keep a list of the different cats you see or meet, paste pictures, or make quick sketches of the kittens.

NEXT STEPS

Hopefully, the pages of this book have given you inspiration and ideas for how to spend more time with your cat and explore doing new things together. My hope is that you and your cat are feeling inspired to keep playing, training, and exploring! Ideas for the future include:

PLAY

Play is such a simple yet essential activity for our cats. Now that you are finished with the book, don't forget to take time out of your daily life to play with your cat and provide them with access to toys. As you've seen through the activities in this book, you don't have to spend a lot of money to keep your cat entertained with toys, games, and activities.

While reading this book and doing these activities, did you learn anything about your cat's play style or their approach to play?

_____

_____

_____

COOPERATIVE CARE TRAINING/HUSBANDRY SKILLS

If you and your cat have had fun with the activities in this book and are looking for new goals, you may want to explore cooperative care and husbandry skills. This training modality involves the same skill set that modern zookeepers utilize to help our cat's big relatives, like tigers and lions, learn to willingly participate in veterinary visits. The same skills can be used at home to teach your cat to opt into husbandry routines like fur brushing, ear cleaning, and nail trimming. You can also teach your cat to willingly present parts of their body for exams at home, or in the vet clinic!

Fear Free Pets is a wonderful organization and resource for cat owners who want to learn more about helping make vet visits and grooming less stressful for their cats. They also has a directory to help you find a Fear Free-certified vet clinic near you, and to gain training techniques you can start using at home. Another resource is Cooperative Care Certification, which has a wealth of information and learning modules to support you in learning more about how to involve your cat as a consenting and active participant in grooming.

FIND A COMMUNITY OF CAT TRAINERS

If you are surrounded by people who are dismissive or look at you weird when you talk about providing enrichment to your cat or spending more time training your cat, you need new friends! Seriously though, shifting your community to include more people who understand the importance of providing enrichment for cats is a good idea. A great way to do this is to build connections with other cat guardians who are training cats!

There are a number of people, both professionals and just loving cat guardians, who are connecting with each other in groups on social media. This can be a great way to make connections with other cat lovers around the world who are providing enrichment activities for their cats, focusing on reducing stress while handling and training their cats!

A good place to start is the Clicker Expo Conference. This is an annual conference that occurs in various places around the United States (and, for the past several years, virtually), bringing together trainers, behavior experts, and pet guardians of all kinds of species (not just dogs!) to discuss and learn about training. This conference has been a wonderful resource for connecting with cat lovers and trainers!

TAKE AN ONLINE CLASS

If you've done the activities in this book and are looking for more ideas for what to teach, you and your cat can always take a class together! There might not be cat training classes in your local community, but online classes are a great opportunity to take your training to the next level. Especially if you are feeling a bit stuck trying to teach a skill to your cat or aren't quite sure how to work on a new skill, working with a trainer can help the learning process make more sense for you and your cat.

On a personal level, I am always happy to work with cat lovers as part of my trick coaching and can help cat lovers earn trick titles with their cats virtually from anywhere in the world. I work with animal/handler teams remotely and have contact information on my website. I have a training group on Facebook at "Tricks in the City" (same name as my dog training book). The group is very welcoming to learners of all species, especially cats!

CAT ENRICHMENT ACTIVITIES

By now, you and your cat will have been able to explore a wide variety of enrichment activities and you probably have a pretty good idea of the things your cat enjoys doing. Moving forward, try to find time in your daily life to incorporate these, and more enrichment activities, into your cat's daily life. From making mealtime a game or activity, to turning off the television and spending time pulling out cat toys, there are so many ways to make your cat's day more interesting. Following hashtags for feline enrichment on social media and joining social media groups focused on cat enrichment can be a great way to find new and innovative ways to entertain your cats and improve their overall quality of life!

ACKNOWLEDGEMENTS

Thank you so much to all the cat experts and cat lovers who I have learned from. Special thank you to authors and artists Zazie Todd and Lili Chin—I love that we all have cat books releasing at the same time. I want to thank my editors at cat-centered publications who I have written for over the years. Thank you to the Cat Writers Association for my 2021 Muse Award for my article "Tricks Are for Kitty" (first published in *Catster Magazine*). Thank you to my trick coaching clients and members of my online training group "Tricks in the City." I also want to thank the entire Mango team for your enthusiasm putting this book together.

Thank you to my partner Kestryl, the real cat person in our family, for your support and encouragement. Most of all, thank you so much for all the cats I have shared my life with, who have taught me everything I know about how to play, train, and have fun with cats. Thank you to the cats of my childhood: Buttermilk, Socks, Coco, Sugar, Tux, Magic, and the cats I've shared my life with as an adult: Zoey, Sierra, Noirchat, and the coauthor of this book, Thing!

ABOUT THE AUTHOR

Sassafras Lowrey is a celebrated author and cat lover who has written for pet lifestyle magazines for over a decade. Sassafras's books have been honored by the American Library Association, the Lambda Literary Foundation, and the Dog Writers Association of America. Sassafras is a 2021 winner of a Cat Writers Association Muse Medallion winner for their article "Tricks Are for Kitty" in *Caster Magazine*. Sassafras's pet training articles have appeared in the *New York Times*, *Wired* magazine, *Apartment Therapy*, and numerous other publications. Sassafras lives and writes in Portland, Oregon, with their partner, giant dog, and mischievous cat. Learn more at SassafrasLowrey.com.

Mango Publishing, established in 2014, publishes an eclectic list of books by diverse authors—both new and established voices—on topics ranging from business, personal growth, women's empowerment, LGBTQ studies, health, and spirituality to history, popular culture, time management, decluttering, lifestyle, mental wellness, aging, and sustainable living. We were recently named 2019 and 2020's #1 fastest growing independent publisher by *Publishers Weekly*. Our success is driven by our main goal, which is to publish high quality books that will entertain readers as well as make a positive difference in their lives.

Our readers are our most important resource; we value your input, suggestions, and ideas. We'd love to hear from you—after all, we are publishing books for you!

Please stay in touch with us and follow us at:

Facebook: Mango Publishing
Twitter: @MangoPublishing
Instagram: @MangoPublishing
LinkedIn: Mango Publishing
Pinterest: Mango Publishing
Newsletter: mangopublishinggroup.com/newsletter

Join us on Mango's journey to reinvent publishing, one book at a time.